Helping with Spiritual Emergencies:
Guiding the Psychonaut through
Conversion, Visions, Near Death,
Ayahuasca, Rising Kundalini, and Oneness
with the Universe

By

Robert Nelson

ISBN-13: 978-1501044540
ISBN-10: 1501044540

Sauntering Press

Also available for Kindle on Amazon.com

Also by the Author

Ayahuasca Journey (Kindle)
Driving as a Spiritual Discipline (Kindle)
Colonel Henry Lawrence Kinney: A Texas Hero (Kindle)
Magical, Mystical, Mysterious Jellyfish (Kindle)
The Persian Roots of World Civilization (Kindle)
Enemy of the Saints: The Biography of Governor Lilburn W.
Boggs of Missouri (Publish America)

Contact author at drbobnelson@gmail.com

Additional books can be purchased at Amazon.com

Dedicated to all my teachers and clients.
Special thanks to Don Jose Campos, Arturo Mena
and to my greatest teacher, lover, friend, fellow
adventurer, and guide
– Behnaz Esfehani

Table of Contents

Foreword

Mystical experiences and altered states of consciousness have been a part of my life since childhood. After thirty years experience as a psychotherapist I can look back and identify spontaneous trances and various anomalous experiences from my first memory to this present day.

Raised in a little country church I experienced different types of altered states in the worship service. Drawn to religion I was drawn from a young age to explore the worship of many traditions. I have visited and worshipped with most Christian denominations and with many non-Christian religions as well. As an adult I served for a time in the United States Army as a Chaplain where I found more resources for my interest in religion but more importantly where I was privileged to counsel with soldiers of many faiths and to learn from other chaplains as well.

I have been a counselor or therapist for over thirty years. Beginning as a psych tech in a mental hospital I worked as a counselor, case manager, school counselor, career counselor, crisis counselor, chaplain, mobile crisis worker, intake counselor, crisis director, clinical director, and director at various locations in the United States and overseas. I have also been a trainer, supervisor, and college instructor.

During my career I have discovered that spiritual experiences are fairly kind and play a major role in the lives of people to provide comfort, guidance, and major learning. I have seen miracles worked by faith and great healing brought through sacred teachings. As a minister and chaplain I have many times been in awe over the

1

resilience and strength people gain from their religions and spiritual paths.

I have also witnessed unusual things. There was the woman and her husband who came to me because they were being oppressed by a vampire. There have been demons invoked through a vortex in a man's backyard. Another man was plagued by vampires. Many people have been bothered by spirits of various kinds. There was the woman who had a son who was visited by a dwarf like those in fairy tales. There have been several who came to me because of voodoo curses. There have been a distressingly large number of children who have been visited by a "dark man" not unlike those I had seen myself when younger. As a missionary in Korea three other missionaries and I saw the same dark form vanish into thin air one night.

I have dealt with many whose path had brought them to a spiritual emergence or a spiritual emergency. For some, their values and choices were called into question. Some of them made dramatic changes – leaving marriages and jobs to enter completely new paths. Others struggled for years or made poor choices. Some suffered from misunderstanding and others caused them to be incarcerated and medicated because they did not recognize their emergence for what it was. In some cases I have been able to help at the time of the crisis. At other times I was there years later to help reconstruct their lives.

Later in life I was privileged to experience some of the entheogenic plants of Peru and Mexico. At this point I have been in over thirty ayahuasca ceremonies as well as a number of ceremonies with San Pedro, Peyote, and other entheogens. This has been extremely important to my development spiritually both as an individual and as a therapist. It has resulted in significant personality changes as well as great increases in my understanding of myself, the world, and the transcendent world in which we live.

At some point one of our friends in the ayahuasca community encouraged my wife, who is an intuitive healer, and myself to do something for those who needed counseling or support following ceremonies. It has been our privilege to provide counseling on a donation basis for a number of people who have had questions, struggles, and issues following entheogenic experiences. Some have had a spiritual crisis. Some simply had questions about their feelings and thoughts. Others were concerned about their experiences and wondered if they were losing their minds. Others were struggling with issues that were not directly related to the medicinal plants but which were possibly triggered by the plant. Others struggled with issues first raised years ago but not yet resolved. These experiences have been some of the most interesting and rewarding in my career.

This works continues. I am now involved with the Spiritual Emergency Network and I have an active private practice. My wife and I move in many interesting circles that include shamans, healers, herbalists, yogis and yoginis, mages, and seekers of many kinds. Our circle of friends has grown to an international level with communications on multiple levels.

There are too many people to acknowledge or thank. Chief among them is my wife, Behnaz Esfehani. She is a light to the world. Don Jose Campos is my friend and mentor. We love him deeply and are forever grateful for his power, wisdom and music. Arturo Mena, my brother and friend, is with me every day through his inspired compassionate music. Of course there are so many other friends who have helped us through a casual word, a loving message, or by holding the space with us.

Included among these are the friends of a lifetime. We are all products of unexpected relationships. Finally there are my clients. I have learned more from them about human psychology and behavior than I have ever learned from a psychology book or class. Most of all I am grateful for the love which seems to permeate all of existence and the healing effect it has had on so many lives including my own.

Introduction

Nothing in this book is particularly new. As long as there have been humans there have been spiritual experiences and emergencies — not by that name of course, but spiritual emergencies nonetheless. We can read about them in our earliest literature. *Gilgamesh*, for example, struggles with communications from gods and goddesses, the relationship of humanity with nature, and the search for immortality. Those are eternal themes in the world's oldest known literature. Much later, but still ancient, is the *Iliad* which describes visions and interactions with gods that at times wreak havoc on the lives of the mortals involved. Then there are the ancient scriptures of the Persians including the *Zend Avesta* and those of their cousins the Aryans of India, most notably the *Rg Veda*. The ancient scriptures are books about people struggling with the problems of life in the context and with the influence of divine revelation and personal spiritual struggle. The story of the ancient Iranian prophet, Zarathustra, is one of the earliest records of a spiritual emergence. Another is the story of Arjuna's spiritual emergency and Krishna's intervention told of in the *Bhagavad Gita.*

Of course it would be unreasonable to assume that spiritual experiences only began with writing — or cities, or agriculture. It appears rather that spirituality and religious behaviors may have been part of being human as long as there have been humans — perhaps even earlier. Some have hypothesized that the emergence of true Homo sapiens was actually the emergence of Homo religiosus. But even without conjecture, we find hard evidence of religious or spiritual behaviors — cave drawings indicating rituals and shamans, burials indicating beliefs in afterlife and the numinous nature of animals and humans, as well as sculptures, icons, altars. And, we have cultural and anthropological evidence which makes it clear that pre-literate societies have myths and rituals associated with spirituality and religion. The myths of the Greeks, Romans, Persians, Egyptians, Indians, Chinese, Celts and others were clearly a lengthy oral tradition that flowed eventually into literature. In other preliterate societies these spiritual artifacts have been captured at times by anthropologists and early observers.

So, spiritual emergence and personal transformation is ancient – possibly as ancient as human existence. A spiritual emergence is a transformative experience which occurs through initiation or as a result of spiritual experiences or disciplines. At times the transformation can be difficult and disruptive to the point that it becomes a spiritual emergency (Grof & Grof, 1989). This and the general struggle of existence and survival led to specialists in helping – shamans, curanderos, yogis, seers, oracles, gurus, prophets, priests, and later even later counselors, therapists, philosophers, and even physicians.

The technologies of helping no matter how new they might seem can be found in the ancient world. Shamans certainly dealt with the same sort of issues that plague modern humanity. The ancient scriptures address timeless issues with direction and advice that remain profound even in the age of internet and texting. Yogis, prophets, gurus and priests provided direction, healing, and insight long before the invention of Psychology or psychiatry. People healed and received healing through music and drama, through play and action, through ritual and prayer, through suggestion, support, advice, and guidance long before the current proliferation of therapies and theories. Late in the ancient world but long before the birth of modern psychotherapy in the fifth century BCE, the rhetorician Antiphon of Athens started a practice in Corinth where he promised to heal with words.

So nothing in this book is particularly new but the world as it continues to change seems surprisingly new for each of us in our individual life. We each discover the nature of life, the meaning of existence, the transcendence of the seemingly ordinary, or we don't. We each must find the values, beliefs, actions – the path that will lead to a fulfilling life or we can remain unfulfilled, hollow, and shallow. We each in our own life in our own way must deal with loneliness, struggles, losses, death, pain, struggle, conflict as well as with connection, success, triumph, birth, pleasure, beauty, and ecstasy. No matter how large the collective data base becomes we each traverse this mortal path individually. We can access at times the wisdom of ancients or even the wisdom of the Divine but ultimately we must walk our own path. It is for this reason that the ancient questions and challenges are always new.

Nothing in this book is particularly new but each day the world is new again. Each day we must meet with the questions, struggles, and challenges of life. Each day we are called on to transcend the ordinary world, to grow in wisdom and compassion. Or, we can fail to meet the challenge and give way to our lesser side.

Some of us have chosen to walk a path that involves us in helping others or as the scriptures might say – serving others. We may have chosen to become counselors, therapists, social workers, ministers, teachers, or priests. We may have chosen to serve while remaining unseen as clerks, bankers, truck drivers, or some other type of worker. Others serve in other ways -- intuitive

7

healers, massage therapists, acupuncturists, nurses; the specific label is not as important as the choice to help others.

The purpose of this book is to give you more tools and understanding. It is not intended to redefine the field of psychotherapy or to promote yet another theory of psychology. It is intended instead to provide you with practical tools and understanding which you can use to help others who may be dealing with spiritual difficulties – regardless of the type or trigger of the crisis or the theology of the person in crisis or yourself.

This book grew out of my experience as a mental health professional. I have been privileged to work with many different types of people, cultures, and religions. During my career I have also benefited from the wisdom and teachings of colleagues and client. I am also especially indebted to a number of great thinkers and scholars whose writings have had an impact on my life and practice. These include William James, Milton Erickson, Terence McKenna among a long list of greats. I am especially indebted to Stan and Christina Grof.

More recently I have been privileged to work with the "ayahuasca community" – people who through various venues have experienced the powerful effects of ayahuasca or other entheogenic plants. My wife and I have been encouraged to take on this role as a support to this particular group in our community. At the same time we have become participants in different circles and communities including various tribal people, religions, and lifestyles. This has provided us with opportunities to step outside our own little world while providing assistance to a greater variety of people.

We are fortunate in being able to provide support and crisis intervention for people experiencing a spiritual crisis. These have included but not been limited to those using entheogenic plants. Our growing circles include others whose crisis has been triggered by experiences with magic, voodoo, meditation, yoga, as well as more traditionally Western paths of spiritual seeking such as mainstream Christian churches, Mormons, Spiritualists, Muslims, Jews, and atheists. It has also resulted in our own increased spiritual awareness along with its application to "non-spiritual" issues such as death, births, life-changes, and relationships.

Support in attaining optimal resolution and integration during a spiritual crisis is part of the social context in traditional cultures where entheogens are used but that does not mean that Western cultures are deprived of such support. Depending on the person's social network there are likely to be groups and individuals who support the individual's spiritual goals and interests. There may be people available who can provide guidance and crisis intervention that is consistent with a spiritual crisis.

If such resources are not available then it might be useful for the groups involved to create such a support system. Most people would expect churches to have ministers who are trained in helping with spiritual emergencies. The same is true for helping agencies such as shelters where it would be reasonable to expect there to be social workers or other professional helpers present to help with spiritual emergencies. Unfortunately, in most cases the support available to help with spiritual emergencies is less than adequate.

Training is an important step to take to improve the situation. Few counselors, therapists, or social workers receive training on providing assistance during spiritual emergencies either on a graduate or post-graduate level. Even ministers, regardless of the religion, do not routinely receive such training. Many are not even required to have any training in counseling – not even pastoral counseling. Not surprisingly the level of support varies greatly ranging from ministers with training and degrees in counseling and advanced training in such fields as Clinical Pastoral Education to those who address every issue with a call to repentance or "say a prayer, read two scriptures and call me in the morning".

Formal institutions must address this issue within their own institutional missions and resources. There is, however, a large segment of society that lies outside those institutions. There is a large segment of society that is unchurched – that is, not identified with a specific religion or denomination. Many of these have an active spiritual life based on a variety of resources. Some may belong to informal groups. Others may be lone practitioners who identify with any number of traditions including Eastern religions. Various New Age and non-traditional people may belong on the periphery of a number of groups but still actively involved as spiritual seekers.

Since this is not an academic book or a book on theory, feel free to follow your intuitions when reading. Feel free to skip around. It is okay to sample different sections and explore where you feel drawn. I hope you will start with the next section which deals with Crisis intervention for a spiritual emergency but I will not be offended if you feel led to begin somewhere else. (In fact, I won't even know.) And, if you find something with which you do not agree or which your intuition, experience, or theology does not feel comfortable then feel free to listen to your own guidance. Just let it be done with integrity and compassion. What more could we expect from ourselves?

Chapter One - Crisis Intervention

As common as words such as "trauma", "crisis" and "suicide prevention" are today, it might be surprising to learn that the field of crisis intervention is relatively new. The first suicide prevention center was established in 1906 in New York City – the National Save a Life League. Now there are suicide prevention centers, crisis lines, mobile crisis teams, and even for-profit suicide lines. It has become an industry in the United States. But even today most crisis situations are encountered first, not by mental health professionals, but by ministers, police, firefighters, EMTs and just ordinary people – family, friends, neighbors, and co-workers.

In 1943 the Coconut Grove fire in Boston led Lindemann (1944) and his colleagues at the Massachusetts General Hospital to develop the concept of crisis intervention. Over the past seventy years this has expanded into a specialty with its own journals, organizations and, of course, legions of academics and college courses. But the specialty is still young and like too much of the mental health profession it remains theoretical to the academics while those in the field must too often learn by experience – or not at all.

One of the main purposes of crisis intervention is to ensure the immediate safety of the people involved. In the immediate crisis we do not want anyone to get hurt by themselves, by someone else, or through inappropriate behaviors in risky settings. It is for this reason that law enforcement personnel, firefighters or other emergency responders must often be in the forefront of such situations. A crisis is not an appropriate place to be doing in-depth talk therapy.

It is not unusual however for mental health professionals (and other "crisis workers" like ministers, educators, and social service workers) to be placed in a situation where they must deal with threats of suicide or violence. It is therefore important for them to know how to assess and de-escalate such volatile situations or at least maintain the safety of all concerned until law enforcement assistance is available. We will discuss some of these principles later.

First, let us define crisis. It is often defined as a situation in which a person's usual resources are unavailable or not working. From this definition we might see the goal of crisis intervention to be resource mobilization or the development of self-efficacy or self-reliance. It can also be seen as a situation in which the person's balance or homeostasis has been disturbed. Using these or similar definitions leads to understanding the goal of crisis intervention as being to restore equilibrium or to stabilize the person or situation.

Although such definitions have proliferated and resulted in many models of crisis with multiple-stepped models of intervention, few of them are truly useful to the helper who is dealing directly in real life with a person in crisis. Some are just too theoretical and complex undoubtedly considered elegant in some university setting but of little practical use. They range from six-stage models to 10-stage models. Others may be too idealistic or even too romanticized to have immediate use.

This lack of utility is the result of several factors. Perhaps the most prominent factor is the disconnect between academics and practitioners. Journals, textbooks and college courses are the realm of academics. Take a look (or an intensive review) of the journals of professional helpers – whether professional counselors, psychologists, or social workers you will find that the overwhelming majority of all articles published are published by academics with little connection to the world of practice. Experiences and views from practitioners in the field are a rarity. Even those academics who refer to their clinical experience will be found to have nothing but a small "practice on the side" or perhaps a pre-academic career as a practicing clinician. They seldom experience the pressures, limitations, or risks involved for those who practice full-time. This lack of connection means that the research done often has no relevance to the needs of the practitioner. It may even be trivial.

Another factor is the failure of the helping professions to rigorously examine their fields and respond to information. They repeat the same myths they learned and when new information is presented there is a strong resistance to changing programs and techniques. You are just as likely to hear the same popular myths and misinformation about mental health in a mental health clinic that you would hear on a television talk show.

For example, Critical Incident Stress Debriefing (CISD) is a popular approach to traumatic events. It is a process that is to occur within twenty four to seventy two hours after a traumatic event. It takes from three to four hours and involves facilitators who assist the "victims" to relate their stories. The facilitators then describe the symptoms of PTSD that the victims can expect to experience and encourage on-going therapy. Research shows that those who are debriefed are much more likely to show symptoms of PTSD at a thirteen month follow-up than are those who do not get a debriefing. Most improve but those who receive no debriefing and no treatment also improve (Regehr, 2001). Given that information we might wonder at the existence of on-going CISD. We might

13

wonder even more at the on-going training and proliferation of CISD.

Another problem with many fields – not just the mental health field – is the problem of "cloning the text" which was identified by Steven Gould in his essay "The Case of the Creeping Fox Terrier Clone" (Gould, 1992, pp. 155-167). In the essay Gould points out how some "facts" in scientific textbooks are actually only repetitions of statements made without confirmation or verification. This results at times in things that "everyone knows" which are in fact not true. But even though not true, they are repeated and the repetition alone gives them credibility. An example of this is the well-known fact that "the Eskimo language has twenty words for snow", or depending on the version of this particular fact, 50 or 100. Although this is repeated often, it is not true. In fact, it has been thoroughly debunked but this does not seem to hinder its use as a cliché in speeches, articles and daily conversation (Martin, 1986). Other examples of this phenomenon are common and include such things as "elephants are afraid of mice", "Obama was born in Kenya", and "We only use 10% of our brains". As Stephen Gould wrote: "Thoughtlessly cloned 'eternal verities' are often false" (Gould, p. 167).

Another example of cloning the text is the common reference to the Chinese word for crisis being made up of the characters for "danger" and "opportunity". John F. Kennedy actually said: "The Chinese use two brush strokes to write the word 'crisis'. One brush stroke stands for danger, the other for opportunity. In a crisis, be aware of the danger – but recognize the opportunity" (Kennedy). While I think this is a wonderful reframe for the word "crisis", it is unfortunately based on misinformation. The Chinese word for "crisis" is wēijī. The first character, not

14

the first brushstroke, means 'danger.' The second character does not mean 'opportunity' but rather something like 'crucial moment'. While this might seem like a trivial point to some, it is not. In addition to being false, it detracts from the credibility of the overall message. It is better to at least try to be precise and accurate rather than to unquestioningly accept and repeat things that "everyone knows".

Crisis intervention with a spiritual emergency

Since the beginning of "crisis intervention" there have developed a number of approaches. Some of these have developed for specific professions like medical settings, emergency services, chaplain services, nursing, counseling, and law enforcement. There are even specific protocols developed or proposed for settings involving psychedelic drugs, other types of intoxication, withdrawal, raves, Burning Man, Kundalini crisis, Qi gong crisis, and, of course, spiritual emergencies.

In general, crisis intervention requires some sort of assessment, the ability to think quickly and creatively and a greater than normal tolerance for unusual behaviors. The helper in a crisis must stay calm and be flexible enough to help people in crisis increase their own flexibility. Although there may be a need to be directive at times, more often than not the helper is offering alternatives. The goal is to manage the crisis rather than resolve it.

Most crises resolve naturally without outside help but with help the hope is that they will resolve so as to leave the person functioning on a higher level than when the crisis began. This is done not by pushing toward a certain goal but by helping the person in crisis to identify skills and resources while establishing some sort of meaningful context. Spiritual emergencies are non-pathological developmental crises that can result in powerful personal transformations when they are allowed to run their course with the appropriate level of support (Grof & Grof, 1989; Lukoff, 1998; Cortright, 1997; Perry, 1976). The focus is on the here and now. The helpers do not impose their own values but simply assist in the process.

Several models for helping with a spiritual emergency have been offered. One of the more useful was proposed by Arthur Hastings who suggested a seven step model for dealing with parapsychological experiences. He suggested that the person in crisis be helped to describe the experience. The role of the helper at that stage would be to listen and reassure the person in crisis. The next step would be to identify or label the experience and to provide the person in crisis with information about the type of event experienced. The helper then should help the person in crisis to conduct some reality testing and to address any psychological needs. There are other approaches as well.

The following approach to crisis intervention is more general and applicable to any type of setting including general counseling or therapy. It is not a linear process and need not be followed in a step-by-step fashion. It is perfectly permissible to move backward and forward within the process. It can be adapted to most theoretical approaches since its emphasis is not on techniques or interpretations based on specific theoretical models but rather on the process of helping.

A Five Step Process

Crisis intervention for a spiritual crisis or regular emotional crisis follows the same basic format. This is the same format that I teach and use for regular therapy or counseling. I have also taught this format to professional crisis workers, counselors, case managers, and others in clinics and at the university level. Although there are other more elaborate formats available in texts on crisis intervention, this is the one I suggest because it is fairly simple and flexible. It need not be followed rigidly or applied prescriptively to the person being helped. It is just a format – an outline that will help you guide the process as you attempt to help someone deal with a spiritual crisis – or any type of crisis for that matter. In fact, for those of you who are involved in any type of helping whether it be formal psychotherapy, guidance counseling, volunteering at a shelter, pastoral counseling, counseling employees, or helping friends in trouble, you will find that this format can be easily adapted to different situations, clientele, and issues. It consists of five steps: 1. Create the space. 2. Assess. 3. Plan. 4. Implement the plan and 5. Follow up.

While engaging in this process it is important to remember that a crisis can extend over a period of time. Even a psychological crisis can extend over weeks or months (depending on the theoretical framework). A spiritual crisis could last for months or years with the person struggling to find meaning in their experience. If we attempt to force the crisis to a resolution (whether spiritual or psychological) we run the risk of making it worse. In most cases we are better served by taking our time and slowing the process down. Just slowing the process down will usually help the person feel calmer and more secure and will prevent any precipitous actions or decisions.

Create the Space

The first step is to create the space for helping the other person. By space I refer to a physical space where you can both be comfortable, safe, and have a reasonable expectation of privacy. This in no means limits the place to an office setting. An office is certainly appropriate but it could be a living room, a dining room, or even a *maloca* – a ceremonial center. It could be outside under a tree or in a park. During my career as a mental health professional and mobile crisis worker I have had the opportunity of doing crisis intervention in many varied settings including – homes, emergency rooms, hospital rooms, churches, jails, police cars, bridges, roof tops, bars, rifle ranges, camp sites, and farms. The type of situation is not important. The important qualities are that the space be reasonably comfortable, safe, and that it has a reasonable expectation of privacy for both the helper and the person being helped.

In some cases this might take some planning to ensure that such a setting is available. In other cases you can usually make do with a little flexibility. But in most cases there will be an office or other appropriate room where the two of you can talk.

But creating a space is not confined to the physical setting. It also includes the energetic and emotional setting. This can be visualized by imagining yourself welcoming the other person by widening your arms and sending out loving energy. You might actually do this with gestures and words but definitely do it with your energy. The point is to let them know that you are there and you care about them. You want to help. Let them know through words, gestures, and energy that they are welcome, safe, and that you are there to help. Creating such a space is not simply a few words and a single gesture. It involves an ongoing process of assuring, reassuring and sending a message of compassion, love, and caring.

If you can successfully create such a space, the other person will find comfort and acceptance. They will be willing to open up and speak with you honestly about their issues and concerns. And they will be much more receptive to any suggestions you might have. Simply exposing the person in crisis to a space of security, non-judgment, safety, acceptance, compassion and love is healing. The creation of such a space decreases the amount of distress they feel and opens the door to healing and integration.

Part of that message of assurance and of creating a space involves the desire and willingness to listen. This means paying attention – not just with your ears but with your whole being. In one sense this is easy – just listen, but most of us find that we seldom just listen. Instead we are thinking about our response, analyzing and judging what they are saying, thinking about other things that have nothing to do with the conversation. Just listen to what they have to say and accept it at face value. This is part of creating the space and it is an important step to take to remove obstacles to open communication.

Conducting an assessment

Step 2 is to conduct an assessment together with the person in crisis. This is not a matter of assigning a diagnosis or label to their experience. Nor is it a matter of

19

determining the truth of their experience. Such an approach tends to challenge and devalue their experience. Besides it is irrelevant. Experiences are experiences. The fact that they have experienced something is all that matters.

Have them talk about the experience if they wish. Some will want to but others will find it difficult or impossible to describe what they have experienced. Spiritual experiences are after all by definition often ineffable. More important to the assessment is to help them to identify the problem.

What is the problem?

How is it a problem?

What would you like to do?

How does this impact on what you want to do?

How does it make you feel?

But a complete assessment is not just problem definition. It also includes an assessment of what is good. This includes the positive impact of the experience, personal strengths, options, resources, and skills.

If you limit your assessment to what hurts, what's wrong, or what's broken then you have nowhere to go. That is basically the conventional allopathic medical model – find a disease and then throw medications at it. A crisis is not a disease; it is a step, a moment in a potentially transformative experience. To help people in crisis you must help them recognize strengths as well as weaknesses. You must help them find a way to resolve the crisis so that they can move to a higher level of functioning. This may involve helping them see that their feelings and thoughts are normal for this type of situation but it will definitely involve helping them identify strengths, skills, desires, and values that they can use to move forward.

In a way it is similar to having a flat tire. Suppose I find a flat tire on my car. I could experience a crisis especially if I have a tight schedule or if my personal resources have been drained by stress. I could get angry at the car and hit it and swear at it. I could kick the tire. I could get angry at myself for allowing this to happen. I can focus more on the problem and try to determine what caused it. I could take it to ridiculous lengths and critique the whole history and development of automobiles, vulcanized rubber, the substandard transportation system. None of these actions will solve the problem. I will just get more frustrated, more focused on the problem, and probably angrier.

To solve the problem of the flat tire I must first define the problem: the tire is flat and I can't drive the car. Problem definition has nothing to do with how it happened or what I should have done. Once I have a clear definition of the problem – the tire is flat and I can't drive the car – then I can assess for resources, possible solutions, and options. So, I have a jack, a tire tool, a spare tire and I know how to change a tire. I've got roadside assistance on my car insurance and I have a phone. Notice that how I define the problem will impact on my options. If I define the main problem as being unable to drive the car when I need to be somewhere in 15 minutes then my focus will not be on changing the tire. My focus will be on getting a ride, calling a taxi, rescheduling an appointment, or some other solution. In any case assessment involves clearly defining the problem along with identifying resources, options, and possible solutions.

While a clear definition of the problem is essential, identifying strengths, resources, options, and possible solutions is by far the most important part of the assessment phase. Sometimes this stage alone will bring resolution to the crisis simply by shifting the focus onto possible solutions and giving hope. Sometimes just taking a clear look at the situation along with potential solutions provides enough of a change in perception that the person in crisis moves to integration.

Develop a plan

Step 3 is to develop a plan. We have created a space where the person in crisis feels safe, welcome, and free to speak. We continue to create this space throughout the process of crisis intervention. This is not a rigid process with strict boundaries. It is a fluid process that can move back and forth but which is built on that relationship established by creating a space of acceptance and compassion. Then we define the problem and identify resources, options, and possible solutions. Next, we take that information and explore those options to determine which one might be most useful and preferable to the person in crisis.

You do not develop the plan. You help the person in crisis develop the plan by helping her or him explore options, resources, and possible solutions. This will also involve exploring wishes, desires, values, intentions, and goals. You cannot make the plan yourself because they must own the plan for themselves. It has to be their plan.

Of course there might be times when as a helper you will have to make a plan and sell it to the person who is in crisis. For instance, imagine that the person you are helping is impaired and unable to drive. You might want to develop a plan for them to get home safely. Possible solutions might be for you to drive them, to call for a ride, or for them to stay overnight. Such plans however will be to take care of your obligations or responsibilities toward the other person; they will not strictly be related to the issue of a spiritual emergency.

Plans can cover a wide range of possibilities. It is not uncommon for spiritual emergencies to lead to drastic changes in one's life. People quit their jobs and find other careers or go on pilgrimages. People have divorces, go back to school, join ashrams, and become activists for causes.

Once the person in crisis has settled or agreed to a plan it is important to be clear about the plan – who is going to do what and when. You will also want them to accept the plan as their plan and commit to following that plan. Still holding the space you have created of openness and acceptance you can motivate them, fine tune the plan by considering possible problems or obstacles, and you can remind them of personal strengths to encourage them. In some cases you may want to help them slow the process down to avoid ill-advised courses of action.

Implement the plan

Step 4 is to implement the plan. Implementation is the responsibility of the person in crisis. It is not your responsibility and any attempt to take over that stage will fail to resolve the crisis. They must own the plan and take the action.

Implementation may also require some sort of follow up which would constitute step 5. This may or may not involve the helper. In many cases the person will do the follow up by evaluating the results of their actions and adjust the plan as needed. In some cases the two of you may agree that you, as part of the plan, will be involved in follow up. This could involve having them report on their progress or it could mean subsequent meetings to continue the process of crisis intervention and support. It could be as often as daily contact or infrequent as annual reports. The important thing is to use the follow up to help the person continue with the plan or to provide additional motivation, encouragement, and help as needed.

More specifics for helping with a spiritual crisis

The basic tool for any emotional or spiritual crisis is the breath. Breathing can be used to increase intensity but also to control the intensity. It is usually a matter of slowing the breathing down. Of course, slowing the breathing down will probably result in deeper breath but the focus of breathing slowly is usually easier. In other words, people might think or feel they are breathing deeply when it is obvious to most observers that their breathing is shallow and rapid. But if you focus on breathing slowly that can be tracked by counting either mentally or with the aid of someone else or a timepiece. A brief mental experiment will demonstrate how important the pace of the breathing is to how we feel. In your mind (or outwardly if you prefer), pretend to be anxious, sad, angry, or fearful. Notice how each of these emotional states involves tensing muscles and breathing quickly and shallowly? Now pretend to be comfortable, relaxed, happy, peaceful, loving. Notice the difference in how quickly or slowly you breathe depending on the emotional state you are experiencing. Adjusting your breathing to control or simply to experience an intense emotional experience is a much better approach than that of freezing the process through medications.

Decrease the intensity when the client is overwhelmed. That is, slow it down but don't stop it.

Slow it down to make it gentler and less disorienting. This in turn will allow integration. It begins with the breath.

Related to breath is the repetition of mantras or affirmations. They may already have a mantra practice. You can ask and see if that will be useful. You can introduce a simple mantra like – counting "Breathe, 2, 3, 4" or something else you think might resonate with them.

Help them to re-connect their consciousness with their body. We sometimes think of this as helping them to become grounded. Some things that help with this include eating. Have them eat heavy foods, especially those which are high in protein, fat, or complex carbohydrates. Have them avoid simple carbs, refined foods and stimulants like chocolate and caffeine. If they are able to engage in physical movement, that too can help them reconnect. This can include, if it feels right, walking, running, yoga, gardening, contact with the earth, washing the dishes, sweeping, raking leaves, or light housework.

Contact with nature is also helpful. This would include things like taking a walk, looking at clouds, working outdoors, and breathing fresh air. Step outside. Lie down or twirl until you fall down on the grass. Take your shoes off and walk in the grass. Notice the sensations – the birdsongs, the feel of the wind, the warmth of the sun. All of these and similar actions are very grounding in a crisis.

Another powerful tool for helping with crisis is sleep. Sleep itself seems to have a healing property. During our sleep we process new learning and our mind-body works hard to integrate new information and to heal places where we are holding on to pain. It helps to restore the chemical balance but also refreshes us on multiple levels.

Body work can also be a useful aid in helping someone who is experiencing a crisis – especially a spiritual emergency. Of course, you would want to get permission first. Then any type of bodywork can be useful especially when applied with intuition. This includes massage, acupuncture, acupressure, reflexology, and Reiki. Of course, only a trained professional should provide these modalities. A backrub is not a massage and not everyone who has a picture of a foot in the window is a reflexologist.

Medications should be avoided since they generally stop the process, and they usually require the horrible pathological labels of allopathic medicine which only create problems. On the other hand there are some holistic and nutritional approaches than can be useful. As mentioned above eating is grounding – especially with the right foods. Magnesium in the evening can help them relax. Bach flower remedies and homeopathic remedies can be useful for a number of conditions including anxiety and insomnia. Incidentally, it is interesting how the curanderos who use ayahuasca use agua de florida to help those who are having a hard time during a ceremony. 5-HTP and the amino acid L-theanine can be used to help some people relax. GABA (gamma-aminobutyric acid) can be used as a supplement to relax or to sleep.

Certain herbs such as spearmint and chamomile teas are relaxing. Passion flower is a little stronger as a calming agent. Kava, hops, and skullcap are even more potent. Stronger still is valerian which can be used for sleep and as a tranquilizer. A glass or two of alcohol can be useful and appropriate for some.

In any case, I recommend the services of a trained professional such as a naturopath or homeopath rather than those of Aunt Mabel who happens to know a nurse who read an article in the newspaper. In this regard it is important to remember that allopathic medical doctors receive little, if any, training in holistic or alternative approaches to health including nutrition. So, they would not be the ideal source for information about anything other than what they are trained in — looking for disease — diagnosis, prescribing medications, and cutting things out or off with knives or chemicals. They do emergency care very well but healthcare is not their strong suit.

Things to Avoid during a Spiritual Crisis

The first thing to keep in mind when dealing with any sort of crisis is to slow the process down. You have plenty of time. A crisis is a disruption of the norm and the person in crisis must spend a lot of energy to deal with the crisis. Because of this energy expenditure along with the discomfort of a crisis, it is time-limited. Sooner or later it will end on its own. Your job is not to end the crisis; your job is to help it end in such a manner that when it ends the person will be functioning on a higher level. If you get in a hurry because of your discomfort then you are more likely to rush and push the crisis to a less desirable resolution. Unless there is a life-threatening situation that requires immediate action to prevent physical harm or death, slow the process down.

Even if you must act quickly do so deliberately. Assess the situation before you rush in. Decide what to do before you take action. Take action. Such situations are rare in normal life and so we are usually not prepared for them. Emergency personnel who regularly deal with such situations have protocols that govern their actions and they receive training in these protocols. Such situations are less common for most of us but that is no reason for not giving some thought to what we would do in a real emergency. The fact that emergencies occur at all is a good reason to take a first aid class or to design our own protocols for emergency situations.

To slow the process down during an extended spiritual crisis may require people to vary their personal spiritual practice. It may be a good idea for them to discontinue their inner exploration for a time. They may want to forego practicing yoga, tai chi, qi gong, and meditation until the crisis subsides or at least until they are feeling more grounded.

The purpose of crisis resolution is to deal with the crisis. The purpose is not to solve every issue or problem the person in crisis may face in life. It is not to correct the way they live or to convert them to your philosophy or worldview. Although a crisis can and often does lead to major changes in a person's life, it is not your job to identify and direct that change. Your job is to help them resolve the crisis in such a way that they are functioning better after the crisis than before. If you try to decide for them what and how that change will be, you will most likely fail to provide the optimal help. Crises are personal and lead to unique personal change.

Do not judge a person in crisis. When we are experiencing a crisis we are not performing at our best level. Our usual approaches and solutions are found lacking. We flounder and struggle. Our usual strengths and strategies are found lacking. No one should face judgment at such a point. While it is true that far too many psychiatric diagnoses are made when a person is in crisis, that does not make such diagnoses either helpful or valid. Helpful intervention means acknowledging, accepting, and supporting a person through the crisis experience. There is simply no place for the allopathic medical model and psychopathology when providing help with a spiritual emergency. As Stanislov and Christina Grof wrote: '[i]t is essential that [people dealing with spiritual emergencies] move away from the concept of disease and recognize the healing nature of their crisis' (1989:192).

In any type of crisis, normalization and education can be useful approaches. Let the person in crisis tell their story then help them to understand the story in a context that normalizes their experience instead of pathologizing it. Carl Jung told of an incident involving these principles:

> I vividly recall the case of a professor who
> had a sudden vision and thought he was insane.
> He came to see me in a state of complete panic.
> I simply took a 400-year-old book from the shelf
> and showed him an old woodcut depicting his
> very vision. 'There's no reason for you to believe
> that you're insane,' I said to him. 'They knew about
> your vision 400 years ago.' Whereupon he sat
> down entirely deflated, but once more normal
> (Jung, 1964, p. 69).

Unfortunately most clinicians in the West regardless of their discipline have little if any training in dealing with spiritual emergencies. A survey of Association of Psychology Internship Center training directors found that 83% reported discussions of religious and spiritual issues occurred rarely or never during training. A hundred percent reported receiving no training or education in these areas during their own clinical training (Lukoff, 1998, p. 22).

To abstain from judgment also means not to invalidate a person's experience. A person's experience, especially spiritual experience, is personal and does not require assessment or judgment. A better approach is to listen and acknowledge their experience. You do not have to validate or invalidate the "reality" of the experience but it is helpful to validate the emotions. Arguing with the person in crisis about the reality of an experience is not crisis intervention. It is advocating for your own perceptions or understanding and these will likely have little to do with the perceptions of the person in crisis. To dismiss an experience as "just a dream", "just a hallucination", "just stress" or with other dismissive words is just not helpful. The truth is, the experience whatever it might be, is real; it's a real experience and as such must be processed in order for the person to move forward and integrate relevant learning. Dismissing a spiritual experience as unreal does nothing to help the person in crisis understand, manage, or integrate what could be a transformative experience.

Helping with a crisis means putting aside your own discomfort in order to be there for the person in crisis. I have seen some well-intentioned people actually interfere with or aggravate a person's process (not necessarily even a crisis) because of their own discomfort. It is alright for a person to cry, for example. That is not a crisis; it is a normal process. Let them cry. Just be there for them. It is normal in spiritual emergencies for people to see or hear things that others are not seeing. Just be there for them. Their crisis is not defined by your level of discomfort.

Another error to avoid when helping with a crisis is the temptation to talk too much. Crisis intervention is more about being present, holding positive energy than it is about talking. Talking can be distracting and interfere with the individual's process. It is often self-serving and so detracts from a focus on helping the person in need. In many cases one of the best tools for crisis intervention is to simply be there for them and listen.

Related to limiting the talking is being aware of the overall setting. As a general rule it is a good idea to help the person in crisis to avoid people, locations, and activities that might stimulate their emotions. It is better to decrease stimulation and it makes no difference whether it is positive or negative.

At the very least a person who is experiencing any type of mental distress should be provided with hope. This is often the greatest gift we can give. Be a friend by being present without panic or looking away. Insist that the person you know and love is still alive and present even if temporarily hidden. Refer to their behavior without labeling it as wrong or abnormal. And, accept the possibility that a mental health crisis can co-occur with an authentic spiritual emergency.

With crisis intervention, the idea is to emotionally connect with people. Mentally the focus is on learning about the type of emergency they are experiencing. And whether client or helper, it is important to avoid talking too much.

Spiritually, be there. Avoid too much intervention because you will usually want the process to continue. You may in some cases recommend stopping, decreasing, or changing their meditation routine. This is a very individual area. Determining the direction to take for mindfulness, concentration or other exercises must respect the person's process and intentions. It seldom helps to have someone else decide the direction of an individual's process. Mindfulness is often useful unless the person is too open at the time. You can have the person concentrate on an object such as a flower, candle, or music. It is often useful to pray and focus on the divine but again this is a very individual. In any case continue to monitor the person in crisis.

Chapter Two-Spirituality and Psychotherapy

Spirituality and religion have long been neglected by psychotherapists. Of course a few prominent psychologists have emphasized spiritual processes and values. William James wrote an important study of paranormal and anomalous events – *The Varieties of Religious Experience*. Carl Jung emphasized the importance of religious experience as well and even openly considered esoteric teachings of alchemy, kundalini yoga, and spiritualism. Abraham Maslow taught the importance of profound spiritual experiences which he called "peak experiences" and Viktor Frankl taught the importance of spiritual values with Logotherapy. Milton Erickson transformed and energized therapy with his use of therapeutic hypnosis and altered states of consciousness. Transpersonal Psychology developed to emphasize spiritual values and experiences and the field of Pastoral Counseling was intended to help pastors apply therapeutic tools in their ministry. Carl Rogers' person-centered therapy although not labeled specifically spiritual certainly reflected spiritual values. But despite these exceptions most therapists and psychologists have shied away from spirituality.

Although there are no universally accepted definitions to explain or differentiate spirituality and religion, some understanding is needed. Religion is usually associated with a formal institution. Spirituality on the other hand is more nebulous and is usually characterized by a general feeling or awareness of closeness or connectedness to the sacred. Religion is largely concerned with uniformity of belief and behavior. Spirituality is more private and spontaneous. Religion is concerned with a structure for spirituality which includes conformity of belief (orthodoxy), and conformity of practice (orthopraxy and morality). Spirituality is concerned with personal experience, transcendence, awareness of the sacred and usually results in increases in love and compassion.

Psychologists and psychiatrists do not generally think of themselves as spiritual or religious. In fact many of them have been and are antagonistic to religion and spirituality. Freud actively pathologized religion in several of his works including *Future of an Illusion* where he defined religion as follows: "A system of wishful illusions together with a disavowal of reality, such as we find nowhere else...but in a state of blissful hallucinatory confusion." In the 1976 report *Mysticism: Spiritual Quest or Psychic Disturbance* published by the Group for the Advancement of Psychiatry the same attitude was maintained that religion is an escape, a regression, and a projection of a primitive infantile state (Group for the Advancement of Psychiatry, 1976). Albert Ellis, an influential therapist and creator of Rational Emotive Therapy which contributed to the development of Cognitive Behavioral Therapy said: "Spirit and soul is horseshit of the worst sort. Obviously there are no fairies, no Santa Clauses, no spirits. What there is, is human goals and purposes...But a lot of transcendentalists are utter screwballs" (Ellis, 1980, p. 637). B.F. Skinner, a behaviorist and one of the most important psychologists of the twentieth century dismissed religion as nothing but "an explanatory fiction" and "...superstitious behavior perpetuated by an intermittent reinforcement schedule."

The general population on the other hand whether they identify with a specific church or religion tends to recognize the importance of spirituality in their lives. Belief in prayer, angels, demons, god, and other aspects of spirituality are common in America while psychotherapists

33

largely ignore this significant aspect of the human experience. As one researcher has observed about psychotherapists:

> It is curious that psychologists are so out of step with the general population in this regard. Perhaps the types of people who choose to pursue a career as a psychologist tend to be more secular or less religious or spiritual than the average person seeking their services. Furthermore most psychologists have received essentially no training on how best to work with religious-spiritual clients or related themes deny the course of their professional training. In fact, two thirds of psychologists report that they do not feel competent to integrate religious-spiritual matter into their clinical work (Plante, 2009, p. 11).

Actually many therapists have adamantly opposed religion and the place of religious values in therapy. During my thirty years as a therapist I have frequently been exposed to therapists, social workers, nurses, and psychiatrists who have routinely voiced negative opinions about religion and spirituality. There has been an assumption that if a client is being religious by speaking about beliefs, reading the Bible, meditating, or praying then that client was "hyper-religious". Religion, in other words, has been equated by many therapists as a symptom or contributor to mental illness. Many have taken this position because of their own atheism; since everything must be reduced to chemistry and physics, there can be no spiritual. Anyone who believes then in God, gods, spirits or non-physical events such as prayer, enlightenment, energetic healing, miracles, or ESP must, by definition be delusional.

This being said it is interesting to note that the ethical codes of every major group of therapists or professional helpers require the helper to be aware of social and cultural factors that would affect therapy. This is true for psychiatrists, psychologists, counselors, and social workers (Sansome, et al., 1990; NASW 2001; American Psychological Association 2002; 2014 ACA Code of Ethics). The Association for Spiritual, Ethical, and Religious Values in Counseling (ASERVIC) identified the key competencies for the ethical integration of spirituality into a counseling setting (Cashwell & Young, 2011). These competencies include being able to describe and identify differences between spirituality and religion including basic beliefs of different systems and being able to recognize the centrality of a client's beliefs and their importance to psychological functioning (ASERVIC, 2009). They proposed that competent counselors be open to multiple perspectives and that they have the ability to suspend their own values especially if they conflict with the client's. Of course this includes being respectful of religious and spiritual systems and authorities. Competent counselors are also expected to actively explore their own beliefs, attitudes and values about religion and spirituality. Counselors without such self-awareness may create unneeded distress for themselves and their clients. Self-awareness is additionally essential for therapists to be able to identify the limits of their understanding of the client's perspective, resources, and to allow counselors to be aware of when referrals to more competent therapists or religious specialists are appropriate.

Fundamentalistic materialism is counter to the beliefs of the great majority of people – including the great majority of those who seek out the help of therapists. It presents a great obstacle to the performance of competent therapy. The competent practice of therapy presupposes the therapist's ability to connect with, respect, and utilize the beliefs and worldview of the client to facilitate healing and change. As the psychologist Allen Bergin has written:

> Treatment approaches devoid of spiritual sensitivity may provide an alien values framework…. A majority of the population probably prefers an orientation to counseling and psychotherapy that is sympathetic, or at least sensitive, to a spiritual perspective (Bergin, 2004, p. 82).
>
> Ignorance of spiritual constructs and experience predispose a therapist to misjudge, misinterpret, misunderstand, mismanage, or neglect important segments of a client's life which may impact significantly on adjustment or growth (Bergin and Payne, 1991).

Many therapists avoid spiritual and religious issues (Nelson, Manning Kirk, Ane, & Serres, 2011). Most counselor education programs give only cursory training in relation to religious issues, if they address them at all (Rose, Westefeld, & Ansley, 2008). Yet, the majority of people in the U.S., "more than two thirds…consider personal spiritual practices to be an important part of their daily lives" (Walker, Gorsuch, and Tan, 2004, p. 70) and more than 90% of those polled believe in God or some higher power (Cashwell & Young, 2011). One study determined that over half of the clients reported that they prefer discussing spiritual and religious concerns in the counseling setting (Rose et al, 2008).

A therapist who is antagonistic to religion and spirituality is not merely incompetent and unethical but possibly harmful. At the very least the failure to attend to the spiritual and religious concerns of clients is a limitation in conventional psychotherapy and research (Bergin and Jensen, 1990; Shafranske and Maloney, 1990; Allman, De La Roch, Elkins, et al, 1992; Larson, Pattison, Blazer, et al, 1986). M. Scott Peck has addressed this danger in *The Road Less Traveled:*

> Psychiatrists and psychotherapists who have simplistic attitudes toward religion are likely to do a disservice to some of their patients. This will be true if they regard all religion as good or healthy. It will also be true if they throw out the baby with the bath water and regard all religion as sickness or the Enemy. And, finally it will be true if in the face of the complexity of the matter they withdraw themselves from dealing at all with the religious issues of their patients, hiding behind a cloak of such total objectivity that they do not consider it to be their role to be, themselves, in any way spiritually or religiously involved. For their patients often need their involvement. I do not mean to imply that they should forsake their objectivity, or that balancing their objectivity with their own spirituality is an easy matter. It is not. To the contrary, my plea would be that psychotherapists of all kinds should push themselves to become not less involved but rather more sophisticated in religious matters than they frequently are (Peck, 1978, pp. 224-225).

Another problem with the fundamentalistic materialism of modern psychiatry is that it runs counter to the scientific approach. A scientific approach requires an open and honest consideration of all data – including data that runs counter to our beliefs and hypotheses. It is startling just how dogmatic many therapists are when it comes to spirituality and religious practice. Dr. David Larson has commented on this dogmatism:

> What is perhaps most surprising about these negative opinions of religion's effect on mental health is the startling absence of empirical evidence to support these   views. Indeed, the same scientists who were trained to accept or reject a hypothesis based on hard data seem to rely solely on their own opinions and biases when assessing the effect of religion on health. (David Larson in Levin and Koening, 2005,   p. 19).

Most clients of psychotherapy claim to be spiritual or religious or both. They either consider the two to be inseparable or they believe they strengthen each other (Cashwell & Young, 2011). Of course there are also those who report being spiritual but not religious, religious but not spiritual, tolerant but indifferent, and agnostic. Regardless of where they stand on the continuum most feel that their beliefs and attitudes are important and they want to talk about them.

Given the near universality of religion in human society it is reasonable to suppose that religion and spirituality serve some sort of social and psychological functions (Reiner, 2007). They have both been shown to have important connections to mental health. Those who report feelings of closeness to deity have less depression, psychological stress, and loneliness along with greater self-esteem and psychosocial competence (Reiner, 2007).

Several studies have found that people who are involved in religious or spiritual practices tend to be healthier both physically and mentally (Dailey, et al, 2011).

In one study two groups received counseling. The first group received religious or spiritual psychotherapies and the other group received secular psychotherapies. The result was that those who received religious or spiritual psychotherapies did better on both psychological and spiritual outcomes than those who received secular psychotherapies (Worthington, et al., 2011).

The importance of spirituality and religion has become increasingly evident as traditional psychology and psychiatry have failed to meet the needs of society. From the mid-twentieth century on, psychology and psychiatry have increasingly adopted the disease-focused, materialistic pharmaceutical approach to mental and emotional problems. They have attempted to reduce human experience to chemistry and physics while discounting the spiritual component. They have labeled any deviance from their perception of normal as mental illness. They have lost faith in human resilience, potential, and hope. They see little possibility for change or growth and turn more and more to pharmaceutical drugs and medical interventions. Insurance companies prefer medication to therapy. Pharmaceutical companies are among the most profitable of big corporations. Psychiatrists have been reduced to a single tool – medication. Therapists are too often reduced to medication managers. And the result is more mental illness than ever in history. There are more of the major mental illnesses in the United States than in any other country. This means more unhappiness and more suffering.

I am confident that at some point this broken system will collapse on its own or be replaced by a more compassionate system. I believe this in part because of the growing importance of religion and spirituality in the lives of the people. Despite the assaults of fundamentalistic materialists religion is not dying in the United States or anywhere else in the world. It is a vibrant and dynamic phenomenon. Despite violent oppression in the Soviet Union and Communist China religion is alive and flourishing. Under the inspired leadership of Pope Francis, Roman Catholicism seems poised for resurgence. Despite the negative images created by radical fundamentalist Muslims, Islam is growing faster than ever and expanding its theology in creative ways. And, those who leave traditional religions are often involved in energetic new forms of spirituality. Some are drawn to the rebirth of pagan traditions such as Wicca which are growing increasingly familiar in today's society. Others find spiritual practice in Ceremonial Magic or Eastern Religions such as Zen Buddhism, Sokka Gakai, Tibetan Buddhism, Taoism, and Sufism. There are others who find something in Hinduism or aspects of Hinduism such as yoga, kirtan and mantra. Sikhism through the teachings of Yogi Bhajan is a growing phenomenon in the United States.

Beyond the existence of extrinsic faith as seen in group membership, evangelizing, rituals, and other aspects of organized religion, our world is experiencing a growth in intrinsic faith as shown by an increase in spiritual phenomena. These include the dramatic increase in the reported number of near-death experiences. This increase is largely due to the ability of modern medical technology to resuscitate people who in previous generations were simply dead. And, knowledge of these experiences has become part of the common knowledge of people everywhere. Additionally, there seems to be an increased awareness of other spiritual phenomena including angels, miraculous healings, and an awareness of the sacredness of Nature and all living things as many become more concerned with the environment.

From the middle of the twentieth century on there has been a significant increase in the awareness of the importance of altered states of consciousness. Various forms of meditation have become common place and even gained some acceptance in the materialistic approaches of allopathic medicine. People in general are much more aware and willing to access the teachings and practices of mindfulness, pranayama, Reiki, kundalini, Holotropic breathing, the Relaxation Response, shamanism, sound healing, hypnosis, and other means of changing from their ordinary state of consciousness. Among the most powerful of these techniques has been an increased knowledge, awareness, and use of entheogens.

Entheogens are medicinal plants traditionally used by shamans to heal, divine, and see visions. They include such plants as ayahuasca, peyote, psilocybin mushrooms, and the San Pedro cactus as well as certain substances which have been derived from plants such as LSD and psilocybin. There are increasing numbers of people who have become aware of these powerful plants. Many even travel to the jungle of Peru or Brazil or the mountains of Ecuador to participate with shamans in rituals involving these powerful plants. We discuss them in greater detail in another chapter.

People grow spiritually for a number of reasons. They might grow spontaneously because of a life-experience that provides them insight or which challenges their dogmas. They may grow through insights gained through study and meditation. They may experience a

41

mystical experience. They could be "born again" through a conversion experience. Some will have their lives changed through trauma or through a near-death experience. Some will experience transformation through the use of entheogenic plants. Regardless of the particular path these spiritual seekers may experience their experience or growth as a crisis. They may become confused or unsure. They may find their values and perceptions totally changed. They may find difficulty integrating their experience with the society in which they live. They may need support and assistance.

To go just a step further, it might be that the complete training of a competent therapist could involve some sort of spiritual emergence. Surely if we were training a Sports Psychologist we might expect some sort of familiar with various activities. We might go so far as to expect personal experience on the part of the psychologist. We certainly could have legitimate doubts about a physically inactive and unfit Sports Psychologist who had not the least familiarity or respect for sports. Is it too much to expect the same of a therapist who deals with religious and spiritual issues? Then when we consider the near universality of religion and spirituality in human experience, can any counselor, therapist, case manager, psychologist, social service worker, nurse, physician, or even psychiatrist be exempted from at least rudimentary knowledge of these realms? To expect a professional helper to provide competent care without at least some awareness of the spiritual and religious needs of the majority of the community they serve would be something like expecting to function in a foreign country without learning the language of the country (but then there are those who have attempted that as well).

To go even further, I would argue that mere intellectual understanding is not sufficient for the therapist who is striving for true competence and even excellence. Experience alone can provide the understanding needed for meaningful connection and empathy. This is the idea behind initiations in various cultures – especially shamanic cultures. The true healer is not just someone who had a class in healing. The true healer is the embodiment of certain principles which have been integrated and lived not merely accepted as a belief. The therapist must be model as well teacher, a guide who is familiar with the path ahead. Jerome Frank, PhD, the author of *Persuasion and Healing" A Comparative Study of Psychotherapy* and former Professor of Psychiatry at Johns Hopkins University went so far as to advocate for psychic skills for psychotherapists:

> My own hunch; which I mention with some
> trepidation, is that the most gifted therapists
> may have telepathic, clairvoyant, or...other
> parapsychological abilities... They may, in
> addition, possess something... that can only be
> termed 'healing power'. Any researcher who
> attempts to study such phenomena risks his
> reputation as a reliable scientist, so their pursuit
> can be recommended only to the most intrepid.
> The rewards, however, may be great (Frank, 1961)

The opinion of Dr. Frank is echoed by that of Terence McKenna the prominent ethnobotanist and advocate of psychedelic experience. McKenna said: "A great psychotherapist to my mind would be a great shaman" (McKenna, 1992, p. 14). Fortunately there are those who see some evidence of a trend toward greater inclusion of spiritual values within the mental health system:

Mental health systems in this country are undergoing a quiet revolution. Former patients and other advocates are working with mental health providers and government agencies to incorporate spirituality into mental healthcare. While the significance of spirituality in substance abuse treatment has been acknowledged for many years due to widespread recognition of the therapeutic value of 12-step programs, this is a new development in the treatment of serious mental disorders such as bipolar disorder and schizophrenia. The incorporation of spirituality into treatment is part of the recovery model which has become widely accepted in the US and around the world. In 1999, the Surgeon General, in a landmark report on mental health, urged that all mental health systems adopt the "recovery model" (Lukoff, 2007, p. 642).

But despite this optimistic appraisal we are still a long way from a complete integration of spiritual values in the treatment of mental illness. This integration will require a much broader revision of the system than simply acknowledging the importance of religion and spirituality in people's lives.

Prerequisites for helping with Spiritual Issues

Anyone who is interested in helping someone with a spiritual issue must consider several things. First, it is not about theology. As a helper it is not your job to develop or point out the correct theology to your client. This is especially true when their belief system is significantly different from yours. Helping people with spiritual issues may involve references to and discussion of belief systems but the process is not intellectual or evangelical. You are not there to correct them or convert them. You are there to help them make sense of their experiences and to integrate their experience with their feelings and behavior.

Secondly, the helper must remember that the most important thing in therapy is the relationship between the helper and the client. A relationship which provides a safe, respectful, nurturing environment will facilitate change. This relationship is far more important than the therapist's theoretical perspective. So, the helper must make efforts to create a relationship where the client can feel safe, respected, nurtured, and loved. If the clients truly feel that you care about them, then they will be much more willing to tell you their thoughts, emotions and concerns. They will also be able to listen and receive suggestions and recommendations.

Third, the helper must maintain a focus on process rather than outcome. Your purpose is not to have the client pursue a specific course of action or to conform to your goals. Your purpose is to engage them in a process of communication that will aid them in their goals, help them to meet their needs, and understand their world.

A process is not a thing that can be held or possessed. It is more like a dance where the music changes and the dancers adapt to these changes. They repeat patterns and they may vary those patterns to create new steps. They interact with each other to create their own unique response to the melody and rhythm. It is not rigid or fixed but rather continually changing and evolving. That is the way of therapy. It is not linear and fixed but rather back-and-forth flowing with the feelings, thoughts, and energy of that moment. It is the process itself that provides healing and growth – not any particular outcome.

Finally, although the process is not about theology, it does involve entering into the world of the person you wish to help. This is done mostly through the development of a therapeutic relationship in which you become informed of the client's perceptions, beliefs, values, and so forth. It may also involve other resources. If the client is from a different culture, for example, then you might wish to do some research about that culture. But then it would be important to clarify with your client your understanding of the culture because we all have our own understanding about cultural values and norms. The most important source will always be the client. The same is true of religious and spiritual values. If a person is coming from a different religion than yours then you might wish to gain some understanding of the beliefs and practices of that religion. But again the ultimate source is the client. Even two people in the same temple or church – in the same pew – may have very different understandings and experience with the same religion. And those same people may have very different beliefs than those taught by the official or orthodox institution.

The counselor must be open to other's religious beliefs and make the counseling session a safe and welcoming place to discuss such matters. Most clients will not automatically assume this is so and will need the therapist's permission before bringing up religious matters. This can be done by asking nonthreatening questions about the person's spiritual and religious background. The failure to ask such questions will result in an incomplete understanding of the client. Some therapists address the subject on the intake form but in my opinion no form or survey can substitute for the one-to-one process. The process is a reflective dialogue that helps the client discover the meaning and role of spiritual and religious issues in their lives. It is not a process of challenging the person's beliefs but rather a matter of exploring and helping the person to understand and integrate values and beliefs.

All religious traditions have concepts that can be useful in any counseling experience. These include such things as hope, forgiveness, faith, compassion, and a variety of ways of letting go and changing perspective including repentance.

But it is not enough to understand religion or spirituality on an intellectual level. The helper must enter the experiential world of spirituality. An attempt must be made to understand empathically through the heart and body what the client is experiencing. This can be aided by exposing oneself to various religious environments. Visit and even participate when possible in rituals, festivals, ceremonies, and worship services. Read the scriptures and listen to the music of other religions. Try to enter into their world and their experience.

Of course another important aspect of entering into another person's religious or spiritual experience is to attend to your own spiritual roots and traditions. If your roots are in Christianity, then respect those roots. Attend worship services, read the scriptures and devotional literature, practice the Christian virtues, and say prayers. If you are Catholic then pray the Rosary, go to Mass, read and follow the teachings of the Church. Regardless of your choice of a spiritual path walk it with integrity. This means much more than simply professing a belief in orthodoxy – correct belief. It means orthopraxy – correct action -- for whatever path you choose. It means much more than remaining at a kindergarten level of understanding and devotion. It means pursuing a fuller understanding and a more profound experience. The most helpful therapists are those who have themselves walked some spiritual path.

And, most important to developing an understanding of another's spiritual world is to ensure that you have your own spiritual world. Beyond belief, dogmas, doctrine, and even practice every religion has a personal practice that is called by various names – devotion, contemplation, meditation are just some of the names to describe this practice. Every path has both an exoteric side – the orthodox and ordinary teachings and practices of the religion, and a mystical esoteric side which involves the individual's personal religious experience. This side appears in Christianity with the contemplative orders and such teachers as St. John of the Cross, St. Teresa of Avila, Meister Eckhart, Hildegard of Bingen, St. Francis, George Fox of the Quakers, and many more. In Islam the mystical side is seen in the Sufis such as Rumi, ibn al'Arabi, al Ghazali and many more. Most, if not all, religions began with mystics such as these including Lao Tzu in Taoism, Gautama Sakyamuni of Buddhism, Mohammad of Islam, and Guru Nanak of Sikhism. It is interesting to note just how widespread these esoteric teachings are – every culture and every religion contains similar mystical teachings.

Take the time to seek out and practice spiritual paths which appeal to you and your roots. Most certainly this will involve some sort of meditation, devotion, and pray. Most likely it will emphasize such teachings and practices as love, compassion and peace. This will help you develop your own inner spiritual strength and understanding. It will open new vistas to you and enable you to provide much more understanding and help to others who are struggling with spiritual issues. But even then it is important to explore the individual's perspective and experience with religion. In the end, religion and spirituality are personal and must be understood individually. As William James said:

> Ought it to be assumed that in all men the mixture of religion with other elements should be identical? Ought it, indeed to be assumed that the lives of all men should show identical religious elements? In other words, is the existence of so many religious types and sects and creeds regrettable? To answer these questions I answer "No" emphatically. And my reason is that I do not see how it is possible that creatures in such different positions and with such different powers as human individuals are, should have exactly the same functions nor should we be expected to work out identical solutions. Each, from his peculiar angle of observation, taking in certain sphere of fact and trouble, which each must deal with in a unique manner. (James, 1902, p. 368).

Spiritual or religious interventions can be either explicit or implicit. An explicit intervention would involve using a spiritual practice in a counseling setting. These could be things like reading religious texts, meditating, or praying in session. Counselors should not assume the role of religious leader or pretend to expertise or training they do not have. But there may be situations when the counselor is familiar with the teachings and practices of a particular religion and is competent to integrate those practices into the counseling session. Implicit interventions do not require an in-depth knowledge but do involve respect and reverence when listening to religious and spiritual themes. Of course either endorsement or judgment of the client's beliefs lies outside the counseling process.

If you choose to pray with those who are experiencing a spiritual emergency or with those who are suffering from mental health issues, it is important to find out their feelings and perceptions of prayer. Do they have a spiritual background that involves prayer? Do they feel the need to pray in a particular format or language? Do they have set prayers which are part of their tradition or do they feel more comfortable with spontaneous prayers? Before praying, ask them if they would like you to pray. Ask them how they would like you to pray. Ask them what we should pray for and if they would like to pray also. Keep the prayer simple and stay within the information the person has provided. Be aware of how the person is doing during the prayer and adapt as needed. Although holding hands during prayer is a common practice, it is generally good policy not to touch anyone without their understanding and consent.

Some traditions practice healing through the laying on of hands but as with prayer in general, it is important for the helper to become familiar with the practice first before discussing it with the client. Then it should be practiced only if it is consistent with the beliefs, understanding and practice. Ask before doing – May I touch you? Would you like to receive the laying on of hands? In most belief systems this ritual will probably be reserved for ministers. As with any religious belief, to incorporate it into therapy requires first respect and understanding. Empty forms used irreverently will probably not be helpful.

Although many psychiatrists, social workers, and counselors avoid reference to or contacts with churches and other faith groups, there is much to be gained by accessing these resources. Faith communities offer a story about the meaning of life in which we can locate our own experience. Their myths, teachings, and rituals provide a container for our conscious and unconscious processes. They provide a sense of identity – either socially with the group or theologically as "child of God" for example. Faith communities help people to hold a place in time and everyday life while opening the door to eternity and bringing greater meaning to life. They provide a moral compass which brings with it an offer of forgiveness and redemption. They offer an assurance of ultimate justice along with a pathway to healing. The rituals of faith communities cover developmental crises. Additionally, faith communities provide a perspective on what happens after death, the experience of community, and the tension that exists between the ideal and the necessity of dealing with daily reality. Such communities also provide an outlet for frustrations, anxieties, and longings.

Cultural blind spots and targeted biases

Even those therapists who consider themselves to be open-minded will frequently reserve a special place in the worldview for Christianity, Catholicism, or specific denominations. They may admire William James and Carl Jung in advocating for the spiritual in human psychology. But when it comes to certain specific religions – in particular those which are dominant or at least visible in their own society – they are less likely to be open and encouraging. It is much more likely that psychological literature with a pro-religious slant will refer to Zen Buddhist, Native American, Hindu, Tibetan Buddhist, or Taoist teachings than to Christian or even Jewish teachings.   Mystical teachings from Judaism, Sufism, or even Christianity are more likely to be mentioned than are mainstream teachings of Judaism, Islam, or Christianity.

Therapists who would never condone religious intolerance for some reason feel free to voice negative opinions about Catholics and mainstream Protestants. Negative references are made such as "Catholic in recovery" or "hyper-religious". Exotic practices from other cultures and religions are romanticized while practices as common as Bible reading and attending church are scrutinized and criticized. Some are quick to point out the scandals and weaknesses of Catholics and other Christians while ignoring the similar issues in ashrams, monasteries, or other religious settings.

It is interesting how techniques such as mindfulness and visualization have been openly borrowed by some schools of therapy, while even acknowledging techniques from Christianity is considered questionable. There are many therapists who seem to consider religious counseling when placed in a Christian context as a questionable approach.

To be consistent, a therapist who claims to value spiritual and religious values must be open to them all. There is no room for bias that deprives the client from potential strengths and resources. The ultimate criteria for determining the value of a particular religious approach for a specific client cannot be determined by bias whether based in theory, culture, or religious orientation. Rather, as William James advocated, religions and spiritual experience must be judged by their effect on people.

Spiritual development

It is fairly well known that humans develop in various ways throughout their lives. Jean Piaget described early childhood development and Erik Erikson described psychosocial development. Lawrence Kohlberg developed a scheme to describe moral development.

Just as we develop physically, mentally, socially, and morally, we also develop spiritually. James Fowler (1981) has identified seven stages of spiritual development. His seven stages describe normal human spiritual development for the individual in relationship to the "universal" or "transcendent." Each stage roughly corresponds to an age range. Stage 0 which some call the Primal or undifferentiated faith stage is from birth to age 2. If a safe environment provides sufficient nurture then the individual develops a sense of trust and safety about the universe and the divine. The inverse is also true. Transition to the next stage begins with integration of thought and language. Stage 1 or the Intuitive-Projective stage last from age 3 to age 7 and mainly learning through experience, stories, images, and people in the environment. Stage 2 or Mythic-Literal stage focuses on school children developing a belief in justice and reciprocity. During this stage anthropomorphic metaphors and symbolic language is often misunderstood and taken literally. Stage 3 or the Synthetic-Conventional stage ranges from adolescence to adulthood. This stage is characterized by conformity to religious authority and the development of a personal identity. Stage 4, the Individuative-Reflective stage, begins in the mid-20s and lasts into the late 30s. It is the state of angst and struggle during which the individual takes personal responsibility for beliefs and increased awareness of conflicts in belief.

Stage 5 or the Conjunctive faith stage has also been referred to as the mid-life crisis. During this stage the individual acknowledges paradox and transcendence relating to the reality behind the symbols of inherited systems. Conflicts from previous stages are resolved with a more complex understanding of multidimensional interdependent truth. Stage 6, the stage of Universalizing faith is the stage where compassion, enlightenment, and universal community are developed.

M. Scott Peck has also described spiritual development in his book *A Different Drum* (1987). Peck uses a four-stage model which is not tied to age but rather relates to the stage in religious belief that leads to or follows a conversion experience. According to Peck's model, a person could convert at any age and later start to question or deepen their faith. His stages begin with Stage I which is characterized by chaos, antisocial behaviors and pretenders. State II, the formal-institutional stage, is characterized by fundamentalism, a need for strict limits and strong binary distinctions, one-sided exclusiveness, limitation of insight to one set of rules, and during which the individual is often rigid, dogmatic, legalistic, and literal. Examples of this stage might include – Osama Bin Laden, Jerry Falwell, Jimmy Swaggart, Benny Hinn, and Pat Robertson. The second stage is followed by Stage III which is that of challenging/skepticism which is like aspects of adolescence. In this stage there is a need to rebel, question, and challenge. It is a period many questions. This is the stage of the skeptic, individual, questioner, atheists, and truth seekers. The next stage is that of the dark night of the soul during which the individual struggles with various aspects of faith and this is followed by a mystical communal stage. According to Peck one stage is not better than another.

The Catholic theologian Friedrich von Hügel (d. 1925) taught that religion consists of three elements which co-exist in balance, tension, or friction in the human soul. Gerard Hughes uses these elements in *The God of Surprises* as the basis for three types of stages of faith related to human psychological development. These types are Institutional (child), Questioning (adolescent), and Mystical (adult) which are similar to Peck's stage II, III, and IV.

Others too have posited various stages of spiritual development. Notable among them are those proposed by Alan Jamieson which he presents in his book *Chrysalis* — as caterpillar, chrysalis, and butterfly.

Roberto Assagioli proposed a transpersonal model of spiritual development. He noted that this process can be difficult:

> Man's spiritual development is a long and hard
> adventure, a journey through strange places full
> of wonders, but also dangers and difficulties. It
> implies radical purification and transmutation, the
> awakening of faculties that were inactive, the
> elevation of the conscience to levels never touched
> before, its expansion in a new inner dimension
> (Assagioli, 2014, p. 1).

Assagioli identifies five critical stages in the process of spiritual realization. The first he describes as a crisis that precedes spiritual development. This happens when an ordinary person with no particular interest in religion or spirituality who accepts at face-value the reality of ordinary life and values experienced a sudden change in his inner life. This could occur from loss of a loved one or for no apparent reason. A sense of unreality and the vainness of ordinary life grows. Uneasiness arises along with a sense of dissatisfaction as though something is missing. This can lead to a sense of inner emptiness, depersonalization, and even to the point of feeling suicidal.

The second stage involves crises which are produced by a spiritual awakening. This may involve the sense of sudden illumination along with energy and great insights. It can involve an awareness of connection with the Divine and with Nature. For some it can involve paranormal experiences such as ESP, visions and voices.

The reactions to such a spiritual awakening constitute the third stage. This involves a resolution that can bring a sense of unity, beauty, holiness of life and expansive love. The personality becomes more pleasant and complete. The person becomes more loving and giving. This phase eventually ends and can be replaced with doubts and criticisms. But no matter how skeptical or cynical the reaction may be the person cannot return to the previous stage.

Eventually the process results in regeneration and the person moves to the next stage. But it is not a linear process. It differs from person to person and requires the person to learn how to deal with the ups and downs of spiritual energy.

According to Assagioli the final stage is the "dark night of the soul" spoken of by Saint John of the Cross. This can involve intense suffering including self-criticism and self-condemnation. Some even feel lost or damned. They may develop disgust for themselves. Such things may occur in earlier stages but not to the same intensity.

For those who wish to provide help to people who are having either a spiritual experience or a spiritual emergency, it could be useful to develop some sort of understanding as to where they are developmentally. It could become apparent that an "emergence" for one person could be something very different for an individual in an earlier stage of development from that of someone who is in a later stage. The same circumstances or precipitant could, in fact, result in a crisis, enlightenment, or little at all depending on the person's stage of development. In fact, their institutional and cultural background will probably color their understanding of the nature of spirituality depending not only on their own developmental stage but also the developmental stage emphasized by their institution or culture.

Resources for learning about spirituality

Written resources for developing your own spirituality and for learning about spirituality and religion specifically and generally are far too numerous to list in any single volume. A good start is to peruse the library shelves and follow your intuitions and curiosity. This "library" research is much enlarged today with access to the internet where there are websites for virtually every spiritual path. The web can also provide you with information about various religious and spiritual paths in your community and you will find that most of them will be very open and courteous to enquiries about their beliefs and practices.

Consider beginning with the basic works of various religions. With about half the world being Christian, a familiarity with the *Bible* might be considered an essential part of any literate person's education. It is the source of many of the images, stories, metaphors and values that are familiar especially, but not exclusively, in the Western world. Additionally, the Old Testament is the foundation document of the Jewish religion and Islam accepts it as a sacred document as well.

The world's second largest religion is Islam and the *Qur'an* is not just a sacred document. It is for many Muslims the very word of God and the central miracle of Islam. It is in a sense the very manifestation of God on par with the Christian conception that Jesus was the incarnation of God. A familiarity with the *Qur'an* is also the key to understanding the mysticism of the Sufis.

There are of course many other sacred books. Each religion has its foundational scriptures beginning with those of the ancient Persians and the religion of Zoroastrianism – the *Avesta,* and those of the closely related and ancient Indian religion – the *Vedas.* Scriptures are many and each of us must make our own decision in selecting which we wish to study. For therapists I would recommend considering the religious preferences of your clientele and choose those that would most benefit your understanding of their world.

Aside from sacred writings there are libraries of devotional and self-help writings which can be of help to the helper. These range from classics by Meister Eckhart and St. John of the Cross to modern books by Deepak Chopra, M. Scott Peck, Yogananda, Pir Inayat Khan, and many others. Since the invasion of Tibet by the Chinese in the 1950s, Tibetan Buddhism has become much more accessible to Westerners. The teachings of His Holiness the Dalai Lama and other Tibetan lamas are wonderful resources on meditation, compassion, emotional control and other important topics of spirituality.

Regardless of what resources you choose I would encourage a reverent and serious study rather than a quick scanning. A superficial review is unlikely to provide you with anything other than a superficial understanding. A shallow understanding is likely to lead to a shallow use like – "Read two scriptures and call me in the morning." A deeper understanding will allow you to reason from the resources in a meaningful context.

The Spiritual Roots of Psychology

Despite the tendency for psychologists and other mental health professionals to be negative toward spiritual issues, there has always been a strong current within the field that is interested in the spiritual aspects of humanity. In fact, to a certain extent psychology is the child of religion and magic. The first "psychologists" were shamans and priests who used a variety of techniques to heal the thoughts, emotions, and soul. Some techniques still in use today were first used by ancient helper. The history of helping people with emotional and mental issues includes the teaching of use of spiritual principles such as compassion, love, forgiveness and also prayer, exorcism, trance, yoga, dance, and magical spells.

The close connection between psychotherapy and earlier methods of helping with what we usually perceive now as psychological problems is highlighted by the use of exorcisms. The so-called witch finder's handbook, *Malleus Maleficarum* by Heinrich Kramer and Joseph Sprenger in 1487, can be perceived as a renaissance ancestor to a book on psychodiagnostics. Much later prominent figures in the history of psychology as Sigmund Freud and Pierre Janet wrote about exorcisms. Alan Gettis wrote: "So we see that exorcism is really a form of psychotherapy, and psychotherapy is really a form of exorcism" (Gettis, 1978, p. 187).

Wilhelm Wundt (1832-1920) who set up the first psychological laboratory in Europe also participated in séances and wrote on the subject. Gustav Fechner was the son of a minister and wrote on religion and metaphysics. Jean-Martin Charcot, the French neurologist, who was influential on Freud, Janet, William James and many others, was also a student of the occult. He had a large collection of rare works on witchcraft and possession and lectured on spiritualism and hysteria. Pierre Janet wrote about his successful treatment of a possessed man.

Sigmund Freud, who still has a profound influence on everyone who studies psychology and even on non-psychologists through his prolific writings, was an atheist but he also wrote about possession and telepathy. His thinking was also influenced Jewish Kabbalah.

Freud's most prominent disciple, Carl Jung, was the son of a minister and also studied with Pierre Janet in Paris. Jung was influenced by Thomas Flournoy who wrote a landmark study of a medium. He went on to do his own study of mediums and wrote his medical dissertation -- On the Psychology and Pathology of So Called Occult Phenomena in 1902. Jung would go on to incorporate ideas from Alchemy and Eastern Religions into his approach to Psychology. In his personal life he also experienced visions and paranormal experiences.

William James, the father of American Psychology, participated in séances and considered spiritual phenomena to be legitimate areas of study for Psychology. His book, *The Varieties of Religious Experience* – is still an important study for anyone interested in psychic phenomena.

A significant number of important figures in the history of psychology and psychotherapy have been ministers or at least interested in religion. This is due in part to the interests ministers have in helping others and in part to the close connection the study of the soul (i.e. psychology) has to ministry.

Psychologists with interests in religion include prominent figures such as Rollo May, Viktor Frankl, and Abraham Maslow who were all involved in the promotion of Existential Psychology. Concerning religion May wrote: "Religion is whatever the individual takes to be his ultimate concern. One's religious attitude is to be found at that point where he has a conviction that there are values in human existence worth living and dying for" (May, 1953, p. 180). Viktor Frankl, a holocaust survivor, developed Logotherapy and wrote *Man's Search for Meaning* which highlights the importance of what are often called spiritual values and existential meaning. Rollo May summarized this focus: "It may sound surprising when I say, on the basis of my own clinical practice as well as that of my psychological and psychiatric colleagues, that the chief problem of people in the middle decade of the twentieth century is emptiness" (May, 1953, p. 13).

Abraham Maslow developed the concept of "peak experiences" – essentially mystical or spiritual experiences as an important aspect of human development. He was important to the development of the so-called "third force" in psychology or Humanistic Psychology as well as Transpersonal Psychology.

Gordon Allport and Erik Erikson are two more prominent psychologists who wrote about religion. Carl Rogers pursued a career in the ministry before switching to Psychology. Norman Vincent Peale was a minister who sought to combine ministry with psychology.

Another minister, Rev. Anton Boisen, was at one point diagnosed as a schizophrenic and then went on to become a therapist. He was important to the development of hospital chaplains and in the education and certification program known as Clinical Pastoral Education. Boisen perceived of certain mental illnesses as being "problems of the soul" and so foreshadowed Transpersonal Psychology and the idea of spiritual emergencies both in theory and in his personal experience.

Transpersonal Psychology

Transpersonal Psychology, although it has no specific tools or method, places a central emphasis on the spiritual. Like some previous therapies such as Adlerian therapy, relationships are important. Transpersonal Psychology teaches that people change through relationships and so all relationships – friends, family, therapist – are important. The therapist is not considered to be the expert; rather, the emphasis is placed on the "client's truth." The therapist does not judge the client's experience. In these and other aspects, Transpersonal Psychology echoes earlier approaches such as Carl Roger's "person-centered" approach, Humanism, and Existentialism.

William James, Carl Jung and Abraham Maslow can also be seen as pioneers to Transpersonal Psychology. Some have even called William James the founder of modern transpersonal psychology. He was the first to use the term "transpersonal" in relation to the field of psychology (Ryan, 2008). He was also a pioneer in parapsychology, studied dissociative states, multiple personality, theories of unconscious, and the effect of meditation. He established relationships with Asian meditation teachers. He pioneered the study of the psychology of mystical experience. He even experimented with psychoactive substances and observed their effect on his own consciousness (Tartakkovskky, 2022). Long before Timothy Leary, Albert Hoffman, Richard Schultes, Gordon

Wasson, Terence McKenna and other psychonauts, William James was exploring the mysteries of human consciousness and altered states of consciousness.

Stanislav Grof is probably the most significant and prolific writer in the field of Transpersonal Psychology. As one of the founders of the field he has provided an important summary of the beginnings of the field:

> In 1967, a small working group including Abraham Maslow, Anthony Sutich, Stanislav Grof, James Fadiman, Miles Vich, and Sonya Margulies met in Menlo Park, California, with the purpose of creating a new psychology that would honor the entire spectrum of human experience, including various non-ordinary states of consciousness. During these discussions, Maslow and Sutich accepted Grof's suggestion and named the new discipline 'transpersonal psychology.' This Term replaced their own original name 'transhumanistic,' or 'reaching beyond Humanistic concerns.' Soon afterwards, they launched the Association of Transpersonal Psychology (ATP), and started the Journal of Transpersonal Psychology. Several years later in 1975, Robert Frager founded the (California) Institute of Transpersonal Psychology in Palo Alto, which has remained at the cutting edge of transpersonal education, research, and therapy for more than three decades. The International Transpersonal Association was launched in 1976 by myself, as its founding president, and Michael Murphy and Richard Price, founders of Esalen Institute (Groff, 2008, pp. 46-54).

Brief Therapy

Although not directly related to crisis intervention, the type of intervention called Brief Therapy has much to offer those who are involved in helping people in crisis. Initially "brief" referred to the length of time involved. In the early twentieth century most approaches to therapy were psychoanalytic and would at times last years. Brief Therapy tends to be just a few sessions but it is about more than the shortness of the therapy. Brief Therapy and Solution-Focused Therapy are just two of the therapies that derive from the almost miraculous approach of Milton Erickson, M.D. who was an important figure in clinical hypnosis and psychotherapy in the twentieth century. His teachings and example influenced a wide-array of important figures in the field of psychotherapy. These include Steve de Shazer, Insoo Kim Berg, and Michele Weiner-Davis who have helped shape Brief Therapy and John Grinder and Richard Bander who developed Neurolinguistic Programming by studying the approaches of master therapist like Erickson, Virginia Satir, and Fritz Perls. These therapists were also influenced by the Mental Research Institute at Palo Alto which was a group formed to study specific issues in psychology and communication. Members of the Mental Research Institute included Jay Haley, Richard Fisch, John Weakland, Donald Jackson, Paul Watzlawick, Virginia Satir, and Gregory Bateson – all of whom made individual contributions to many areas of study including systems approach, strategic therapy, and constructivism. They incorporated and studied specific techniques from Milton Erickson including various hypnotic techniques, utilization, joining with the client, and paradoxical interventions. Anyone who is interested in crisis intervention, or for that matter, psychotherapy can benefit greatly from a study of solution-focused brief therapy.

Positive Psychology

During most of the twentieth century the field of Psychology was focused primarily on pathology. Rather than being the study of the human soul or even the human mind, emotions, and behaviors, it has been largely focused on what is wrong and what label to apply to it. Abraham Maslow who was a prominent figure in the development of Humanistic Psychology, the Third Force in Psychology after Psychoanalysis and Behaviorism, commented on the traditionally negative focus of Psychology:

> The science of psychology has been far more
> successful in the negative than on the positive
> side. It has revealed to us much about man's
> short- comings, his illness, his sins, but little
> about his potentialities, his virtues, his
> achievable aspirations, or his full psychological
> height. It is as if psychology has voluntarily
> restricted itself to only half its rightful jurisdiction,
> and that, the darker, meaner half. (Maslow, 1954,
> p. 354)

Of course, positive psychology had not been totally missing. William James spoke about "healthy mindedness" in *The Varieties of Religious Experience* in which he also explored spiritual aspects of human psychology. The importance James placed on these concepts can be seen in the subtitle of this pivotal work – *A Study in human nature.* According to Maslow who is remembered by many, including non-psychologists, for his hierarchy of needs and the concepts of self-actualization and peak experiences, "Peak experiences are transient moments of self-actualization" (Maslow, 1971, p. 48). He emphasized personal growth and fulfillment and described peak experiences as uplifting, ego-transcending, euphoric mystical experiences that transcend the ego and lead to personal growth. And, like James, Maslow addressed these profound issues in a book concerning human nature.

Otto Rank who broke with Freud was an influence on Carl Rogers, another important figure in the development of Humanistic Psychology and a generation of therapists. Other key figures include Eric Berne who developed Transactional Analysis and Fritz Perls who represented Gestalt Therapy.

Transpersonal Psychology as well contains elements that are similar to the teachings of Positive Psychology. The use of the word "holotropic" as in "holotropic breathing" for "holotropic mind" for one example is an extremely positive frame. The word holotropic means to move toward a state of wholeness (Grof, S., 2013). The Positive Psychology movement we now know grew out of the teachings of Maslow and Humanistic Psychology as well as from James and others but it is usually viewed as beginning with the 1998 American Psychological Association Presidential Address given by Martin E.P. Seligman. Seligman deserves the credit for developing and promoting Positive Psychology as an increasingly important aspect of modern psychology. Another important contributor to this movement is Mihaly Csikszentmihalyi whose book *Flow* emphasizes many of the aspects of Positive Psychology. Here is Seligman and Csikszentmihalyi's description of positive psychology:

> The field of positive psychology at the subjective level is about valued subjective experiences: well-being, contentment, and satisfaction (in the past); hope and optimism (for the future); and flow and

happiness (in the present). At the individual level, it is about positive individual traits: the capacity for love and vocation, courage, interpersonal skill, aesthetic sensibility, perseverance, forgiveness, originality, future mindedness, spirituality, high talent, and wisdom (Seligman & Csikszentmihalyi, 2000, p. 5)

Of course, as with everything else, we cannot confine the principles of Positive Psychology to the recent thoughts of Western scientists. The very same principles can be found from various teachers of many traditions throughout history. Ram Dass, who was formerly the Harvard Psychology professor Richard Alpert, heard the following from his Himalayan guru: "The world is absolutely perfect, including your own dissatisfaction with it, and everything you are trying to do to change it" (quoted in Grof, S. (1990). P. 40).

Philosophical Counseling

Less well known to counselors and therapists is the approach known as Philosophical Counseling. Although proposed in modern times by the philosopher Lou Marinoff, this approach is ancient and compatible with religious values. Pythagoras who is often called the first philosopher was in his own time more of a religious leader and metaphysical healer. He owed a great deal of his knowledge and training to the Persians and possibly the Egyptians. A perusal of any of the great Greek philosophers reveals how they were strongly invested in the religious rites and teachings of their day including reverence for the gods, Many Greek religious cults such as the Eleusian rites, and the Dionysian rites, involved ecstatic activities that cause altered states of consciousness. One of the most famous of the ancient oracles was the Pythia, the oracle at Delphi, who prophesied the miraculous birth of Pythagoras and for whom he was named. Socrates, by the way, spoke openly of his personal *daimon*, an entity who spoke to him and often told him what to do.

Ancient philosophers dealt openly with the issues of alleviating suffering and maximizing happiness. Even today their rigorous teaching provides useful information on living the best life and dealing with the problems of life. Marcus Aurelius among the Stoics wrote plainly and powerfully on these important issues. Epicurus taught that an argument is worthless if it does not alleviate suffering. Epictetus was one of many insightful philosophers who taught much that is still of use to people in the twenty-first century. Boethius wrote his important work in the frame of a vision of the Goddess of Fate. Antiphon of Athens actually opened the first counseling office that we have record of and promised to heal people with his words.

Philosophical counseling involves defining terms and concepts, examining arguments (or as we might say today "thought processes"), exploring assumptions and logical implications along with conflicts and inconsistencies. These are not totally foreign processes to several modern counseling approaches including NLP and Gestalt but they are used with a little more rigor perhaps in a philosophical approach (Marinoff, 1999).

Anton Boisen and Pastoral Counseling

Counseling is not a foreign concept to religion. Priests, pastors, shamans, gurus, and other religious functionaries have functioned as counselors since time immemorial. Depending on their culture and understanding they have helped people to heal emotionally, mentally and spiritually. At times this has involved propitiating the gods, casting out demons, and performing rituals. Quite often it has involved talking, persuading, listening, empathy, changing perspectives, supporting, and other processes that we identify today with counseling or therapy. It should be no surprise then that as the fields of psychology and psychiatry begin to emerge from their infancy pastors and priests began to look to these new fields for tools to help with their ministry.

Anton Boisen experienced a break with reality that led to hospitalization in a mental institution in the early twentieth century. He recovered from the experience and wrote a book *The Exploration of the Inner World* (Boisen, 1936) in which he described his personal experience of dealing with psychosis which he described as a process of religious and spiritual problem solving. He knew that for many of his peers in the hospital the spiritual crisis did not end positively. He also observed that many religious leaders from history had experienced their own spiritual crisis. This led him to explore ways of helping people find better resolutions to their personal spiritual struggle.

His research led him to conclude that there were two types of schizophrenia. One is correctly perceived by mental health professionals as an organic disturbance while the other is a form of spiritual problem-solving used to cope with overwhelming difficulties that do not fit with the person's world view or abilities. The spiritual problem is natural and purposive and the role of the pastor or therapist is not to stop or hinder the process from unfolding but to assist in removing obstacles to allow the process to take its course.

Boisen trained seminary students to work in psychiatric hospitals and led church services with sermons and music intended to help the patients. He organized a patients' choir and supervised the seminarians in finding ways to listen to the patients' spiritual struggles. He encouraged an empathic and friendly relationship instead of the hierarchical relationship favored by many therapists. He led the way for future therapists in thinking of certain mental health issues as spiritual issues that can benefit from a spiritual approach. He is credited with founding the field of Pastoral Counseling.

Other Spiritual approaches to mental illness

One of those to follow in Boisen's steps was a Jungian analyst named John Weir Perry. Perry also considered the psychotic process to be a natural problem solving process related to the breakdown of a person's worldview. Perry (1974) concluded that psychoses are spiritual in nature and that hallucinations and delusions contain mythic and archetypal themes which are powerful and meaningful.

Perry created a group home called Diabasis for people who had experienced a recent onset of psychosis (Perry, 1974; 1999). Only non-mental health professionals were hired to assist because Perry felt that educated clinicians would hamper the process with their preconceptions about schizophrenia. He sought out staff who were open to diverse life experiences and who were open, sociable and good listeners. The staff was involved as caretakers by overseeing cooking, cleaning, and other daily functions as well as acting as therapists. Therapy consisted of listening to the clients and helping them to interpret the powerful spiritual symbols in their hallucinations and delusions. Medication was not used.

Although the program only lasted a few years due to budget restraints in the mental health system, data indicated the approach was successful. The average stay was only 48 days. Severely psychotic clients became coherent within two to six days without medication.

A similar program was started in San Jose, California. The Soteria House ran from 1971-1983 with nonprofessional staff who were chosen because of their lack of exposure to the medical model in mental health treatment. They were trained to consider psychotic experiences as a developmental stage leading to growth and often containing a spiritual component that included mystical experiences. A strong positive relationship between clients and staff that focused on listening and support was central to the program. Only 10% of the clients were ever given medication since medication was believed to interfere with the process of growth (Mosher & Menn, 1979).

When compared with a traditional program, it was found that clients' length of stay was longer at Soteria (166 days versus 28 days in the traditional program). But the Soteria clients recovered in six to eight weeks without medication. An independent two-year follow up between Soteria and a psychiatric hospital it was found that fewer Soteria subjects were using antipsychotic medication and they were much less likely to be using mental health services (Mosher & Menn, 1979).

Lukoff developed a related program which involved twelve weeks of holistic health with social skills training for schizophrenics. The program involved yoga, meditation, mantras, positive visualization and art therapy. Some sessions involved exploring experiences such as shamanic initiation and vision quests. Participants did significantly better than traditional interventions in decreasing symptoms and preventing relapse (Lukoff, Wallace, Liberman & Burke, 1986). The authors were impressed by the positive response to meditation since others had reported that meditation can cause distress in people experiencing psychosis (Walsh & Roche, 1979).

Spiritual and religious approaches to therapy

Bringing spirituality into counseling brings with it insight, hope, and change. But as with any approach there are appropriate application and inappropriate applications. Unless the counselor is trained and credentialed as a religious functionary then he or she should not engage in religious rituals or presume other aspects of a religious role. A therapist, in other words, should not be absolving sins or perform other religious rituals. Care should be taken to avoid an excessive focus on spirituality to the neglect of other forms of healing on the cognitive, emotional or interpersonal levels (Cashwell & Young, 2011). Therapists should avoid "spiritual bypass" which involves the neglect of other approaches along with the use of spirituality to derail the process or to avoid meaningful interactions. An example of this would be saying "God bless you" to avoid confrontation or conflict (Cashwell, Bentley, & Yarborough, 2007).

Although there are those who frame spirituality as good and religion as bad; as in I'm spiritual but not religious. It is important to recognize that any institution, process, or approach can be used competently and meaningfully or incompetently and superficially. Spirituality at its best involves a personal connection with the spiritual or divine. It is an individual experience in which the internal world of the person connects with the transpersonal reality to provide insight, strength, wisdom, and comfort. This is experienced as a mystical experience or as ecstasy. It involves rising above the mundane to experience the transcendent. With this transcendent experience the individual is led to compassion, kindness, and reaching out with love to help the world.

Religion at its best provides a community with common values and interests that is interested in cooperatively working to promote common values and spiritual growth. It provides mutual help, guidelines, direction, ritual, and common beliefs. It provides teachers, ministers, and a safe supportive setting for spiritual exploration and self-improvement. At its worst it is a hierarchal power structure interested in the judgment and control of others both in and outside the community. It is exclusive and elitist as seen by the exclusion of some and the idolizing of a few. The focus is on an empty legalistic approach that values appearances above personal reality. At its worst it is like that of the Pharisees whom Jesus condemned or the Israelites at the time of Isaiah through whom God condemned their sacred rituals as empty because of the absence of real devotion and the ignoring of justice and righteousness.

To merely judge an approach by the words spiritual or religious is therefore inadequate. These words are used to justify a whole range of functional and dysfunctional behaviors. Spiritual can apply to sincere seekers and practitioners of every faith and culture or it can be used to justify doing nothing except yielding to one's whims, instincts, and lack of interest. Religion encompasses some of the greatest and wisest such as Gandhi, Mother Teresa, and Martin Luther King but has and is used by many of the hateful, ignorant, narrow-minded, and bigoted as well. So we must be clear – at least to ourselves – what we mean when we apply these terms to therapy. By all rights that definition must be made by the individual therapist based on experience, growing understanding, and insight derived from personal practice spiritually and/or religiously and of course as a therapist.

Nevertheless we will introduce one possible definition here to help start the process and to give some setting for this discussion. This definition comes from *Handbook of Religion and Health*:

> Religion involves beliefs, practices, and rituals related to the transcendent, where the transcendent is God, Allah, HaSham, or a Higher Power in Western religious traditions, or to Brahman, manifestations of Brahman, Buddha, Dao, or Ultimate Truth/Reality in Eastern traditions... Religion is a multidimensional construct that includes beliefs, behaviors, rituals, and ceremonies that may be held or practiced in private or public settings, but are in some way derived from established traditions that developed over time within a community....
>
> Spirituality is distinguished from all other things – humanism, values, morals, and mental health – by its connection to that which is sacred, the transcendent.... Spirituality includes both a search for the transcendent and the discovery of the transcendent, and so involves traveling along the path that leads from non-consideration to questioning to either staunch non-belief, and if belief, then ultimately to devotion, and finally, surrender (Koenig, King, and Carson, 2012).

Bringing spirituality and religion into the therapy session begins with an awareness of these factors in the person's life. Just as you would want to know about family background, occupation, and personal history, you will want to be aware of the role of spirituality in a person's life. Just being aware and acknowledging the importance of these things in a person's life will enhance your therapeutic relationship and will provide you with additional tools and insights. This information will provide you information about their community, support group, values, interests, and personal resources. Depending on their background and interests such information may provide you with various tools that can be used as homework assignments or at times even in the session. Such tools include meditation which is frequently used in a secular frame by mainstream therapists. Closely associated with meditation is prayer which can be recommended or encouraged as an individual activity or as a group activity. Closely related to prayer and meditation is the rosary for Catholics (*mala* for Hindus, *tasbih* for Muslims). Gaining an understanding of their approach to spirituality and religion may also provide information about their sense of vocation along with their understanding of the purpose and meaning of life. It can also help you understand how they approach an acceptance of self and others, forgiveness, gratitude, kindness, compassion, love, ethical values and behaviors, and any sense they may have of being part of something larger and greater than oneself. Religious beliefs and activity will provide insights about their feelings about volunteerism and charity, ritual, community support, social justice, bibliotherapy (including incorporating scriptures which emphasize therapeutic principles), the sacredness of life, and spiritual models.

These can be used by the therapist in formulating a plan with the client that will facilitate change and improve functioning. Some of this information can become interventions on their own – like bibliotherapy and meditation. Others can be used as motivation or homework to encourage connection with community or higher resources. And much of it can be used as part of a fabric of intervention that will weave a person's values and beliefs into a holistic approach to health, improvement, healing and integration.

An assessment of a person's religious and spiritual background can also provide insight into factors that may lead to spiritual struggles and so need spiritual responses. Karen Kersting (2003) proposes being sensitive to the role of spirituality for emotional issues and assessing a person's sensitivity to introducing religion and spirituality to therapy. Conflicts between behavior and a person's understanding of what is sinful or acceptable may play a role. Some, for example, may perceive that failure in a marriage is evidence of a serious character flaw or failure to live a righteous life. Others might see financial struggles or other difficulties as evidence of punishment for sins. Certain emotional responses such as fear, a sense of powerlessness, anger, resentment, despair, and hopelessness may indicate spiritual struggles and can often benefit from a spiritual frame or response. Other factors that can affect therapy include a person's view of the future, the possibilities of forgiveness, the presence of hope, and the promise of healing.

Religious affiliation is a poor indicator of religious involvement but it is an indicator of activity and belief. It provides information that might relate to other factors that may impact the person.

Much of the spiritual aspect of therapy will involve exploring these factors with the person. It is a matter of looking with them for the promises and strength in their own beliefs and then incorporating these things into their life. The insights from religion can be used to elicit hope, acceptance, understanding, and any number of internal resources and strengths. Of course, it may also be that these beliefs and activities may invoke blessings and healing from supernatural resources – like God. That is certainly not a possibility to be taken lightly or ignored. To me it makes much more sense than placing one's faith in psychotropic medications that are justified to the FDA with only two positive studies even if there are thousands of negative studies (cf. Peter Breggin *Toxic Psychiatry).*

Research into the effectiveness of religious or spiritual shows that Religious Cognitive Behavioral Therapy is better than Cognitive Behavioral Therapy (Koenig, King, and Carson, 2012). Other research shows that psychotherapy with readings from the Quran and Islamic prayer is more effective in the treatment of depression and bereavement in Muslims in Malaysia as compared with traditional therapy (Azhar and Varma, 1995). Spirituality has also been considered as a resource for couple therapy (Anderson and Worthen, 1997).

Another application of spirituality or religion to therapy is group therapy. Spirituality groups have been used effectively in several settings. They are usually be time limited to nine or ten sessions with several sessions devoted to spiritual histories, several more to spiritual gifts, and the rest devoted to coping strategies. They could be devoted to spirituality in general and incorporate material from various traditions or they could be focused around a single approach. Spiritual journaling, readings from inspirational literature or scriptures would also be appropriate. Depending on the makeup of the group there may be an appropriate place for prayer, meditation, or other spiritual practice. The point is not to teach religion or to proselytize but rather to identify strengths, backgrounds, and beliefs and then build on them to increase a person's understanding and ability to cope with situations.

ChapterThree-Problems with Psychopathology

One of the major areas of psychopathology is that of psychosis. This label often involves symptoms such as delusions and hallucinations. Of course, these can occur with a variety of disorders including schizophrenia but also with depression, bipolar disorder, delirium, and other disorders. So we cannot according to the current approach to diagnosis confine them strictly to any one class of disorders nor can we view them as definite indicators of any specific disorder or indeed of the presence of a disorder. Of course the narrow materialistic view of modern psychiatry does not agree with what I have just written. For psychiatry any experience that lies outside their basic assumptions is evidence of psychopathology. As Crowley observes: "This is based on the assumption that we understand the nature of 'reality', and that there is narrow band of 'normal' perception, outside of which there is little useful potential" (2006, p. 1).

Alternative points of view include the idea that there are alternatives to the usual state of consciousness which include unusual perceptions and experiences. Certain aspects of psychopathology such as "psychosis" have even "...been defined as 'any one of several altered states of consciousness, transient or persistent, that prevent integration of sensory or extrasensory information into reality models accepted by the broad consensus of society, and that lead to maladaptive behavior and social sanctions'" (Nelson, 1994; quoted in Crowley p. 1). If we work from different assumptions, we will of course arrive at different conclusions. Marion Hubbard has proposed that schizophrenia is more often a spiritual emergency: "In terms of the transpersonal dimension of the human psyche, so-called 'schizophrenia' is a part of the human condition and a concern of transpersonal psychology. In the conceptual framework of transpersonal psychology, schizophrenia can be understood as a period of crisis involving psychic overload..." (Hubbard, 2009, p. 1.).

A great problem is that the fundamentalist assumptions of psychiatry and psychology leave no room for much that is normal and transcendent in human experience. Stansislav Grof has observed this not just as a problem of misdiagnosis and perceiving the normal as pathology but also as a loss of much in human experience that is transformative. He wrote:

> One of the most important implications of the research of holotropic states ils the realization that many of the conditions, which are currently diagnosed as psychotic and indiscriminately treated by suppressive medication, are actually difficult stages of a radical personality trans-formation and of spiritual opening. If they are correctly understood and supported, these psychospiritual crises can result in emotional and psychosomatic healing, remarkable psychological transformation, and consciousness evolution...
> (Grof, 2009, pp.1-2).

Mainstream psychology and psychiatry leave little room for the consideration of spirituality or religion. Many psychiatrists and psychologists have no religious affiliation or spiritual practice and so are unable to connect with their clients around these issues or to incorporate them into their therapy. When there is discussion of spirituality or religion in conjunction with "schizophrenia" or "psychosis", mainstream journals relegate these factors solely to symptomology and etiology (Brewerton, 1994; Getz, Fleck & Strakowski, 2001; Larson & Larson, 1994; Post, 1992; Siddle, Haddock, Tarrier, & Faragher, 2002). Some mainstream researchers even consider religion and spirituality as exacerbating factors for psychosis (Koenig, McCullough, & Larson, 2001).

This runs counter to the perception of Transpersonal Psychology and many famous psychologists such as William James and Carl Jung. Jung commented eloquently on the emptiness of reductionistic psychology:

> We think we can congratulate ourselves on
> having already reached such a pinnacle of
> clarity, imagining that we have left all these
> phantasmal gods far behind. But what we
> have left behind are only verbal specters, not
> the psychic facts that were responsible for the
> birth of the gods. We are still as much possessed
> today by autonomous psychic contents as if they
> were Olympians. Today they are called phobias,
> obsessions, and so forth; in a word, neurotic
> symptoms. The gods have become diseases; Zeus
> no longer rules Olympus but rather the solar
> plexus, and produces curious specimens for the
> doctor's consulting room, or disorders
> the brains of politicians and journalists who
> unwittingly let loose psychic epidemics on the
> world (Jung in Hollis, 2005, p. 161)

Others consider religion and spirituality to be critical factors in the treatment of psychosis (Lukoff & Lu, 2005; Shorto, 1999). Transpersonal psychologists have described psychosis as a natural developmental process that includes spiritual as well as psychological components (Lukoff, 1988; Perry, 1999; Shorto, 1999). Other researchers have discussed the similarity of psychotic symptoms and spiritual experiences with the implication that they share underlying processes and that full understanding and treatment of psychosis may depend on understanding and appreciating spiritual experiences (Arieti, 1976; Boisen, 1936; Buckley, 1981; James, 1958). In fact, research indicates that psychotic symptoms may occur with spiritual experiences rather than with mental illness (Jackson & Fulford, 1997; Lukoff 1985, 1991, 1996). In one case it was found that four young men became psychotic after studying Jewish mysticism. They experienced hallucinations, social withdrawal, and delusions that were indistinguishable from those experienced reported by many mystics (Greenberg, Witzum, & Buchbinder, 1991).

These cases encourage us to recognize that not all psychotic symptoms actually indicate psychosis. Some are indicators of spiritual experience or spiritual emergency. Of course this is not a major revelation since it has long been recognized that within the field of psychiatry there are no pathognomonic symptoms. That is to say, unlike medical diagnoses where observable and measurable symptoms are present such as broken bones, inflamed tissues, and lab reports, psychiatry infers the presence of mental illness through symptoms but the symptoms are not clearly linked with specific diagnoses. For example, hallucinations might be present with psychosis, depression, mania, or underlying physical issues such as dementia or drug use. Or they could be present with normal people.

This discussion of assumptions and theory may not seem to have much relevance to those readers who are more oriented to practical work with clients. I too have little patience with complex theories or theologies that have little if any practical application. But, they are important because they shape our perspectives. A devout fundamentalist of any faith — Christian, Muslim, Atheist, Materialist, or Psychiatric — is not likely to encounter evidence that runs counter to their faith. This then impacts on how we observe, assess, and treat those we encounter. It also prevents us from receiving corrective feedback. For example, one study of the effectiveness of Critical Stress Debriefing found that it can actually increase symptoms (Regehr, 2001). This is unlikely to have any effect on ongoing grants and programs supporting Critical Incident Stress Debriefing.

Another problem with the field of psychopathology is that it generates more pathology. There is seldom if ever discussion of the benefits of psychopathology or even of improvement or spontaneous remission. Diagnostic labels have become increasingly life sentences. A mental illness has become perceived as something which must be coped with and managed for the rest of one's life. Such illness is expected to get worse and the person with the label is taught to expect to take medications with their side-effects because there is no cure. Karl Menninger however observed: "Some patients have a mental illness and then get well and then they get weller! I mean they get better than they ever were.... This is an extraordinary and little-realized truth" (quoted in Silverman, 1967).

The concept of "delusions" ultimately comes down to one person's belief. If that belief is not accepted by the person whose job is to apply the label (that is, make a diagnosis), then the other person will be labeled delusional. Not surprisingly the mental health field has many stories of people who were assessed as delusional initially only to find that their delusions were in fact, "real". Delusions are not generally held in spite of the evidence but because of evidence but it is not standard procedure within psychiatry to consider evidence which runs counter to the assumptions of psychiatry.

The application of the label "delusion" frequently reduces down to politics and other facets of a person's worldview. So, a conservative might believe that "homosexuals are bad and are contributing to the deterioration of society" while a liberal might believe that "homosexuals are people who are entitled to the rights to which all people are entitled." The conservative might make statements about "real rape" and "voter fraud" while the liberal will advocate for the protection of all people and the rights of everyone to vote. To the conservative the poor might be considered "thieves" who take advantage of the system and the liberal might focus on the need for everyone to contribute and so decry "welfare to the wealthy corporations" and advocate the importance of taking care of everyone in society. The conservative may advocate "trickle down economics" while the liberal is concerned with the growing gap between rich and poor. The conservative may hate government and champion individual liberty while the liberal may encourage cooperation and working together. The conservative may see gun rights as fundamental and essential while the liberals shake their heads at archaic values and the gun lobby's ability to advocate the possession and use of deadly weapons in a civilized country. The self-evident truths of one side are often perceived as madness by the other side.

This is so not just in politics but in many areas of life: Rap v. Country, Chick flicks v. Action flicks, solar power v. oil, big house v. small house, carnivore v. vegetarian. In fact, no matter where you look you will find that false beliefs are common. And false beliefs are, by definition, delusional.

That being the case then it must be admitted that a false belief, in and of itself, is not necessarily evidence of psychopathology. Of course, there are those who would attempt that blanket label against the opposing political party or other groups but such a selectively diagnosis of those who disagree is not a rigorous use of diagnosis. It is not a reasonable criterion for applying a mental health label. Of course, it has been done in the past and it is done now but it is not good science and is certainly not helpful.

A much more reasonable course might be to consider how the person behaves and functions in society. They could believe something demonstrably false like the Flat Earth Society but go to work, function in society, care for a family, and in other ways fit in with society's norms. The fundamental issue again is that modern psychiatry leaves no place in its approach or assumptions for normal human experience much less for the spiritual and transcendent. As Stanislav Grof has written: "Mainstream psychiatrists do not differentiate psychospiritual crises or even episodes of uncomplicated mystical experiences, from serious mental changes, because of their narrow conceptual framework" (Grof, 2009, p. 2).

Mainstream psychiatry also fails to recognize the culture-bound nature of labels. That is to say, they only recognize one culture – mainstream psychiatry. Anything that lies outside that narrow perspective is subject to being labeled pathology. Cross-cultural considerations led Prince (1992) to recognize the importance of culture in considering this issue:

Highly similar mental and behavioral states may

85

be designated psychiatric disorders in some
cultural settings and religious experiences in
others... Within cultures that invest these
unusual states with meaning and provide
the individual experiencing them with
institutional support, at least a proportion of
them may be contained and channeled into
socially valuable roles (p. 289).

On the other hand, there is a growing interest in alternatives to the fundamentalist, materialist, disease-focused, Big Pharma controlled medical system. This interest in alternatives is perhaps nowhere as great as it is in reference to psychiatry. The iatrogenic effects of medical treatment including increased occurrence of diseases and even death are a growing concern. These issues together with growing expense coupled to an increasingly inadequate "Healthcare" system are driving many to question the underlying assumptions of what appears to many to be a broken system. Many of the alternatives being considered are open and even encouraging to spirituality. Stanislav Grof has observed and contributed to this growing interest in spirituality:

In recent decades, we have seen rapidly
growing interest in spiritual matters that leads
to extensive experimentation with ancient,
aboriginal, and modern 'technologies of the
sacred,' consciousness-expanding techniques
that can mediate spiritual opening. Among
them are various shamanic methods, Eastern
meditative practices, use of psychedelic
substances, effective experiential psychotherapies,
and laboratory methods developed by experimental psychiatry. According to public polls, the
number of Americans who have had spiritual

86

experiences significantly increased in the second half of the twentieth century and continues to grow. It seems that this has been accompanied by a parallel increase of psychospiritual crises (Grof, 2009, p. 3).

While psychiatry has tried without success to relegate the thoughts and emotions of human beings to the chemistry of the brain, people have increasingly been seeking meaning. Finding emptiness in owning things, the business of everyday life, and the violence and struggle of soul-less materialistic systems and philosophies, many are turning to religion and spirituality. As Grof observes:

> More and more people seem to realize that genuine spirituality based on profound personal experience is a vitally important dimension of life. In view of the escalating global crisis brought about by the materialistic orientation of Western technological civilization, it has become obvious that we are paying a great price for having rejected spirituality. We have banned from our life a force that nourishes, empowers, and gives meaning to human existence (Grof, 2009, p. 3).

The dehumanizing and demoralizing effects of psychiatry and much of psychology have created generations of people who perceive themselves as fundamentally flawed and in need of medication. This coupled with the negative effects of mass marketing, mindless electronic entertainment, and processed, factory-farmed foods empty of nutrition have created an increasingly obese, inactive, sedated population. The answer? For the system, the answer is more medication, more distraction, more of the same.

> On the individual level, the toll for the loss of spirituality is an impoverished, alienated, and

unfulfilling way of life and an increase of emotional and psychosomatic disorders. On the collective level, the absence of spiritual values leads to strategies of existence that threaten the survival of life on our planet, such as plundering of nonrenewable resources, polluting the natural environment, disturbing ecological balance, and using violence as a principal means of international problem-solving (Grof, 2009, p. 3).

Hallucinations

The other major symptom that is often associated with a diagnosis (label) of psychotic is that of hallucinations – a subject which is closely intertwined with the history of psychiatry and psychopathology.

Psychiatry as a branch of medicine is relatively new. In the late eighteenth century physicians embraced institutionalism as a curative for insanity; this in many ways represents the beginning of psychiatry as a specialty. In fact, the period from 1750 to 1800 can be considered the time of proto-psychiatry. The term "psychiatry" was not even coined until 1808. The prominent figures in the field at the time advocated compassion and seclusion from society for the treatment of the insane. Prominent among these early psychiatrists were William Battie (1704-1776) in London, Vincenzo Chiarugi (1759-1820) in Florence, and Philippe Pinel (1745-1826) in Paris.

The second wave of psychiatrists included Jean-Etienne-Dominique Esquirol (1722-1840) who was Pinel's favorite student and the most influential psychiatrist in Europe. He fought to imbue psychiatry with some scientific legitimacy and advocated for the treatment of the insane with kindness. In 1817 Esquirol introduced the first formal course of clinical instruction in France. He almost single-handedly laid the foundation for diagnostics with several landmark papers and his identification of mental disorders by their symptoms. He collected and revised these papers into his 1838 book *Des Maladies Mentales*, the most important psychiatric text of the age. He also introduced the word "hallucination" into the medical lexicon and so began the debate of whether hallucinations are intrinsically pathological.

His students included some of the most prominent psychiatrists of the day. These included Louis François Lélut (1804-1877) who wrote *In Search of Analogies Between Madness and Reason*. He concluded that there is no distinct dividing line between sanity and insanity. Another of Esquirol's students was Alexandre Brierre de Boismont (1798-1881) who wrote *On Hallucinations* in 1845 in which he argued against the idea of considering auditory hallucinations as evidence of pathology.

The nineteenth century witnessed great efforts to make new medical names – a movement which continued into the twentieth. Emil Kraepelin developed the term "dementia praecox" in the late nineteenth century to describe a type of psychosis. The Swiss psychiatrist Eugen Bleuler replaced dementia praecox with the term "schizophrenia" in 1908 not to describe a split personality but the split between psychological functions like thinking, memory, and perception. After World War II, Kurt Schneider created a checklist of 1st rank symptoms of schizophrenia. This was translated from German to English in the 1950s and became the basis for the World Health Organization's classification as well as for the Diagnostic and Statistics Manual. Each of these diagnoses included auditory hallucinations as a symptom of psychosis.

Those who insist on labeling any unusual experience a symptom of pathology argue circularly – hallucinations cannot represent a "real" experience therefore they are symptoms. There can be no clairvoyance, clairaudience, ESP, or other psi phenomena, therefore those who report such things are hallucinating and are therefore experiencing some sort of mental illness. Of course, to make this argument they must ignore large amounts of data concerning hearing voices and other phenomena. This approach denies support to those who have anomalous experiences. But psychiatry and mainstream psychopathology does not have the tools to correct the situation: "Both Western religion and science lack the cognitive models and language to describe such states in a nuanced way, just as Western culture fails to support those experiencing these states with a viable cultural language" (Douglas-Klotz, 2001, p. 71).

They argue that since the majority of patients on psych meds for auditory hallucinations experience a reduction and sometimes cessation of voices, the voices were symptoms (Tien, p. 12). That is, since the medication reduces hallucinations then the medications were nothing more than a brain phenomenon. Of course, we could alter or remove normal hearing or normal vision through medication but no one would argue that there was no "real" hearing or vision. We might as well argue from anesthesia that feeling and the things we feel are delusional. This sort of argument reveals just how non-scientific some of the so-called science of psychiatry actually is.

Carl Jung observed the tendency to pathologize much of human behavior. In his study on UFOs he observed:

Nowadays people who have an experience of

this kind are more likely to go running to the
doctor or psychiatrist than to the theologian.
I have more than once been consulted by people
who were terrified by their dreams and visions.
They took them for symptoms of mental illness,
possibly heralding insanity, whereas in reality they
were 'dreams sent by God', real and genuine
religious experience that collided with a mind
unprepared, ignorant, and profoundly prejudiced.
In this matter there is little choice today: anything
out of the ordinary can only be pathological, for
that abstraction, the 'statistical average', counts as
the ultimate truth, and not reality. All feeling for
value is repressed in the interests of a narrow
intellect and biased reason" (Jung, 1958, P. 43).

Jung was willing to take a more scientific view of
human experience than are the modern practitioners of
psychiatry and psychology who simply ignore or label as
mental illness anything that lies outside the norm of
human experience and much that lies within the norm.
Not surprisingly Jung preferred non-pathological labels: As
Carl Jung observed in his study of UFOs: "I prefer the term
'vision' to 'hallucination', because the latter bears the
stamp of a pathological concept, whereas a vision is a
phenomenon that is by no means peculiar to pathological
states" (Jung, 1958, P. 19). Jung also observed that such
experiences are within the normal range of human
experience:

Even people who are entirely *compos mentis*
and in full possession of their senses can
sometimes see things that do not exist. I do not
know what the explanation is of such happenings.
It is very possible that they are less rare than I am
inclined to suppose. For as a rule we do not verify

things we have 'seen with our own eyes', and so we never get to know that actually they did not exist (Jung, 1958, P. 20).

He also preferred to include all that is human rather than restrict the study of psychology to a narrow sample of what people do.

Since psychology touches man on the practical side, it cannot be satisfied with averages, because these only give information about his general behavior. Instead, it has to turn its attention to the individual exceptions, which are murdered by statistics. The human soul attains its true meaning not in the average but in the unique, and this does not count in a scientific procedure. Rhine's experiments have taught us, if practical experience has not already done so, that the improbable does occur, and that our picture of the world only tallies with reality when the improbable has a place in it. This point of view is anathema to the exclusively scientific attitude, despite the fact that without exceptions there would be no statistics at all. Moreover, in actual reality the exceptions are almost more important than the rule (Jung, 1958, P. 95)

As we can see from the large-scale research cited above, auditory hallucinations are part of the human experience. In a 1971 study, Welsh doctor Devi Rees questioned 300 people who had recently lost a spouse. Thirteen percent had heard the voice of their dead husband or wife, ten percent had held a conversation with them. Eighty percent reported the process as pleasurable and said it helped with mourning (Rees, 1971). Daniel B. Smith in his book *Muses, Madmen, and Prophets:*

Rethinking The History, Science, and Meaning of Auditory Hallucination states:

> What is even less commonly realized is that
> auditory hallucinations extend to people who are
> not suffering from any pathology at all – that is,
> people hear voices without any distress or
> impairment in functioning. Sometimes people
> even enjoy the experience (Smith, 2007, p. 8).

In the mid-1980s, Foundation Resonance, a self-help organization of people who hear voices was organized. The purpose of the organization is in part to advocate for the normality of voice-hearing. It is connected with the 1993 book – *Accepting Voices* which was written by Marius Romme and Sandra Escher Smith.

Taken from a longer historical view we might conclude that revelation and inspiration have become symptoms of pathology. The names of voice-hearers compose some of the greatest and most influential minds in history. Included are Socrates, the Hebrew prophets, Jesus, Mohammad, John Wesley, and many more.

The list becomes even more impressive when we expand it to include mystical experiences, visual hallucinations, and channeling – all dismissed as pathology by the fundamentalist materialists as some sort of misfiring of the brain. Consider just a few of these visionaries; Friedrich August von Kekule had a vision of the chemical formula of benzene while gazing at the fireplace coals. This vision was the birth of organic chemistry. Dimitri Mendeleev envisioned the periodic table of elements while lying in bed exhausted. Niels Bohr envisioned the planetary model of the atom. Heisenberg's basic principles of quantum physics began with a mystical-like experience. Otto Loewi, the discovered of the chemical transmission of neuronal impulses, was a visionary who won a Nobel Prize for it. William Blake, artist and poet, wrote his poetry as though taking dictation. Mozart said he often found symphonies in complete form in his head.

Visions

Many spiritual experiences are accompanied by visions or what psychiatry calls hallucinations. The conventional psychiatric model leaves no room for normal hallucinations or normal anything for that matter. An hallucination is to psychiatry a symptom of mental illness, delirium or some other problem. Hallucinations are, by definition, unreal sensory experiences – seeing or hearing things that are not there. Visions are a preferable term since they allow for the non-pathological experience of non-ordinary or transcendent perceptions.

Voice hearers have included characters in the *Iliad*, Socrates, the Biblical prophets, St. Augustine, St. Thomas Aquinas, Hildegard of Bingen, Teresa of Avila, Martin Luther, George Fox, John Bunyan, John Milton, Antoinette Bourignon, William Blake, Joseph Smith and many more poets, religious leaders, and even common people. Thomas à Kempis, the first century German monk who wrote *Imitation Christi*, said: "Blessed are those ears that receive the whispers of the divine voice, and listen not to the whisperings of the world. Blessed indeed are those ears that hearken not to the voice which soundeth outwardly, but unto the truth which teacheth inwardly."(quoted in Smith, p. 97). But, the *DSM* makes no allowance for visions, inspiration, or any nonpathological occurrence of voices because the field of psychiatry has decided ahead of time that there is nothing outside chemistry and physics. Humanity has been stripped of

94

thought, consciousness, transcendence; indeed psychiatry has no room for the mental or spiritual aspects of humanity.

On the other hand shamans, mystics, and religious teachers have always differentiated between visions and madness. St. Teresa of Avila in 1577 in *The Interior Castle* differentiated between divine visions and those caused by illness. She hoped to prevent the Inquisition from acting against nuns by attributing their visions to sickness (*enferma*) since one cannot be held accountable for illness. Ironically, today the danger to visionaries is reversed. It is most likely that a person who has visions will be imprisoned in a hospital, medicated and discounted because of being ill – modern psychiatry is much less lenient than the Spanish Inquisition which actually had allowance for divine visions.

The word "hallucination" was introduced to the medical lexicon by Esquirol, the prominent French psychiatrist, in the nineteenth century. He was responsible for almost single-handedly laying the foundation of psychiatric diagnosis and his 1838 book *Des Maladies Mentales* was the most important psychiatric text of that age. But the concept of hallucination as intrinsically pathological was not universally accepted on its introduction. One of Esquirol's students, Louis François Lélut argued *In Search of Analogies Between Madness and Reason* that there is no clear dividing line between madness and reason. Another of Esquirol's students, Alexandre Brierre de Boismont argued against voices as evidence of pathology in 1845 with his book *On Hallucinations*. But eventually the term hallucination became accepted by psychiatry as a symptom of mental illness as it is today. Revelation and inspiration have become symptoms and pathology. Carl Jung expressed his opinion on this terminology:

> I prefer the term 'vision' to 'hallucination', because the latter bears the stamp of a pathological concept, whereas a vision is a phenomenon that is by no means peculiar to pathological states (Jung, 1958, P. 19).
>
> Even people who are entirely *compos mentis* and in full possession of their senses can sometimes see things that do not exist. I do not know what the explanation is of such happenings. It is very possible that they are less rare than I am inclined to suppose. For as a rule we do not verify things we have 'seen with our own eyes', and so we never get to know that actually they did not exist (Jung, 1958, P. 20)

In a 1971 study, Welsh doctor Devi Rees questioned 300 people who had recently lost a spouse. Thirteen percent had heard the voice of dead husband or wife, ten percent had held a conversation with them. Eighty percent reported the process as pleasurable (Smith, p. 8). It helped with mourning (Rees, 1971).

In the late nineteenth century, the Society for Psychical Research questioned 17,000 adults as to whether they had ever heard a voice – excluding the physically or mentally unstable they found that 3.3% had had vivid auditory hallucinations at some point in life. Fifteen percent reported voices on multiple occasions (Sidgwick, et al, 1897). Allen Tien, a psychiatrist at Johns Hopkins U. replicated the study in 1991 by collecting data from over 18,500 people as part of a study for NIMH. Results were similar to an earlier study as for percentages. In the earlier study most voice-hearers were in their twenties. In the later study most were middle aged and elderly. Two-thirds reported feeling no distress and had no plans to seek professional help. Tien's study was the most comprehensive survey of hallucination in the general population conducted so far.

Spirituality vs. Psychiatry and the Medical Model

Sixty-percent of APA member psychologists surveyed "...reported that clients often expressed their personal experiences in religious language, and that at least 1 in 6 of their patients presented issues which directly involve religion or spirituality" (Shafranske and Maloney, 1990, p. 1). Seventy-two percent of psychologists have at some time addressed religious or spiritual values with clients during treatment (Lannert, 1991). In a sample of psychologists, psychiatrists, marriage and family therapists, and social workers, 29% agreed that religious issues are important to the treatment of all or many of their clients (Bergin & Jensen, 1990). According to Anderson and Young: "All clinicians inevitably face the challenge of treating patients with religious troubles and preoccupations" (Anderson & Young, 1988, p. 532).

In a survey of Association of Psychology Internship Centers training directors, 83% reported that discussions of religion and spiritual issues in training occurred rarely or never. One hundred percent indicated that they themselves had received no education or training in religion or spiritual issues relating to therapy and they stated that little was being done at their internship sites to address these issues in clinical training (Lannert, 1991). In a national study of APA member psychologists it was found that 85% had rarely or never discussed religion during their own training (Shafranske & Maloney, 1990).

No wonder one study concluded that lack of training is the norm throughout mental health professions (Sansome, Khatain, & Rodenhouser, 1990). And yet all the mental health professions have published ethical guidelines that require them to be aware of social and cultural factors in their treatment of clients. "Cultural competency" has in fact become a fashionable, even popular, subject in some organizations without any significant growing awareness in the importance of religion and spirituality as a social and cultural factor.

The increased interest of some psychologists in the spiritual aspect of human experience led to the development of Humanistic Psychology and Transpersonal Psychology. Unfortunately the field as a whole continued to be dominated by allopathic, disease-focused psychiatry for whom religion tends to be ignored or even discounted. Eventually issues concerning religion and spirituality were included in the "bible" of mental health – the *Diagnostic and Statistical Manual of Mental Disorders* (DSM-IV-TR). This can be seen as an advance in the sense that spiritual issues are at least acknowledged but the focus is negative. The Religious or Spiritual Problem category was included as a "V-code" which is technically not a mental illness because of the frequent occurrence of such issues in clinical practice. The category has been carried over to the DSM-V which was published in 2013 and described as follows:

> This category can be used when the focus of clinical attention is a religious or spiritual problem. Examples include distressing experiences that involve loss or questioning of faith, problems associated with conversion to a new faith, or questioning of spiritual values that may not

necessarily be related to an organized church or religious institution (DSM-IV, p. 725).

In truth part of the problem of assessing a spiritual emergence is that superficially it can appear as a mental health problem. A person experiencing a spiritual emergence might be disorganized in speech and behavior and report visions which are perceived by mental health professionals as hallucinations. They may speak of unusual beliefs which will be interpreted as delusions. They may also behave strangely and experience wide swings of mood together with changes of consciousness. For this reason several researchers have proposed criteria for distinguishing between psychosis and a spiritual experience with psychotic features (Grof and Grof, 1989; Agosin, 1992; Lukoff, 1985). Lukoff proposes four criteria including good premorbid functioning, acute onset of symptoms – within three months, a stressful precipitant that can account for the acute symptoms, and a positive exploratory attitude toward the experience (Lukoff, 1985).

One of the reasons for the superficiality between psychosis and spiritual emergence along with the prevalence of religious mystical symbolism in schizophrenic speech is that they share common processes. Carl Jung pointed to the universality of these processes through common symbols in schizophrenia, mysticism, alchemy, religion, and alchemy that he believed pointed to a collective unconscious. There are those who would argue that all schizophrenia reflects a spiritual struggle or crisis. Certainly this is the view of some shamanic traditions and other spiritual beliefs.

The differences of opinion about the nature of psychosis, mystical states, and spiritual emergence have led to differences in opinion about appropriate treatment. Some theorists have argued that a transpersonal approach is not appropriate for psychotic individuals (Jung, 1960; Wilber, 1984; Grof and Grof, 1989). Boisen who was mentioned earlier as the founder of Pastoral Counseling believed spiritual approaches for the spiritually based psychoses but not for the organically based psychoses. Lukoff and others say that transpersonal psychotherapy is appropriate for even serious psychotic disorders (Lukoff, 1996).

In any case assessment of a situation must go beyond the routine psychiatric history to include a person's spiritual experiences, developmental level, and premorbid functioning. In an ideal world, the helper conducting the assessment would be sensitive to cultural, religious, spiritual, and even paranormal factors. But we probably have a way to go before most therapists would admit to intuitive or psychic skills even if they did have them. But it is not outrageous to ponder training for mental health professionals in other approaches to healing, psychic skills, and even experience with shamanic approaches and entheogenic plants.

Consider the following passage which is a transcription of a dialogue with Nisargadatta Maharaj, a poor cigarette vendor in India.

> Look, my thumb touches my forefinger. Both
> touch and are touched. When my attention is on
> the thumb, the thumb is the feeler and the
> forefinger—the [felt]. Shift the focus of
> attention and the relationship is reversed. I
> find that somehow, by shifting the focus of
> attention, I   become the very thing I look at
> and experience the kind of consciousness it has;
> I become the inner witness of the thing. I call this
> capacity of entering other focal points of
> consciousness—love; you may give it any

name you like. Love says: 'I am everything.'
Wisdom says: 'I am nothing.' Between the two
my life flows. Since at any point of time and space
I can be both the subject and object of experience,
I express it by saying that I am both, and neither,
and beyond both (Nisargadatta, 1973).

This passage reflects the loss of ordinary ego boundaries in a feeling of connectedness or union that is common to the mystical experience and common to many religious traditions. It raises profound questions about the nature of reality.   In his later life Nisargadatta was regarded by many as enlightened but if this passage were a little less organized or expressed in the wrong setting it could be dismissed as the mutterings of a schizophrenic. This similarity may reflect common processes underlying the psychotic and mystical states.   At least that is the approach of several theorists (Washburn, 1994; Nelson, 1994).

The problem of psychiatric diagnoses extends way beyond spiritual issues and deserves a brief review. The history of psychopathology is to a large extent a history of psychiatry and to a lesser extent a history of psychology. Although the study of the human mind and behavior has ancient roots it began in earnest in the eighteenth century and especially in the nineteenth century.   From its beginning it has been fraught with political, economic, and social problems. For example, before the Civil War slaves who tried to escape from slavery could be assigned the psychiatric diagnosis of drapetomania. Women have and still are frequently victims of psychiatric labels – just because of their gender. And, homophobic beliefs still color the perceptions of many psychodiagnosticians.

By the late nineteenth century there were only six diagnoses that were generally accepted and used. These were mania, melancholia, dementia, idiocy, hysteria, and neurasthenia. In 1917 the Committee on Statistics in what is now the American Psychiatric Association with the National Committee on Mental Hygiene developed the *Statistical Manual for the Use of Institutions for the Insane*. The pamphlet had 22 diagnoses and included a subsection on standard nomenclature. In 1943 during World War II an Army committee issued a War Department Technical Bulletin that later become the first *Diagnostics and Statistics Manual* in 1952. It consisted of 130 pages and 106 diagnoses. The *DSM II* was published in 1968. It had 134 pages and 182 disorders.

In 1980 the *DSM III* was published. It used more colloquial English to describe disorders rather than assuming a psychodynamic etiology. It deleted neurosis and introduced a multiaxial format. It was also heavily politicized. It was an attempt to facilitate pharmaceutical regulation. It introduced ego-dystonic homosexuality as opposed to just homosexuality. It had 494 pages and 265 diagnoses and it led to the medicalization of much of the population who may not have had a mental disorder. It was compiled by committees who voted on what type of disorders they wanted included, a process of consensus rather than research. Although widely used, it can be seen as a failure in many ways. It had no effect on regulating pharmaceutical decisions which have little or no relationship to the medication psychiatrists choose. These decisions are much more influenced by the marketing activities of pharmaceutical companies than any rigorous diagnosis.

DSM III-R was published with 567 pages and 292 diagnoses. In 1994 *DSM IV* increased to 886 pages with

297 diagnoses. *DSM IV-TR* was issued in 2000 with few changes. These increases in size and the number of diagnoses do not indicate newly discovered diseases or newly developed means of treatment. They are the results of committees brainstorming about labels.

After many years of promised improvements including lab tests, *DSM V* was published in 2013. There were no lab tests or other empirical findings to support the diagnoses. The *DSM* does not identify causes. The day before its publication the National Institute of Mental Health issued a statement that it would no longer fund research based only on *DSM* categories. NIMH, which provides 1.5 billion dollars for mental research, based its decision on the lack of validity of the *DSM*. "Lack of validity" means in everyday speech that the categories are not true. The diagnoses are not discrete which is to say there are no symptoms which clearly indicate a specific diagnosis. Anger for example could indicate ADHD, Bipolar, Borderline Personality Disorder, Narcissistic Personality Disorder, PTSD, Substance Abuse, Grief, Intermittent Explosive Disorder, and six other *DSM* categories.

DSM V has been criticized for the undue influence of the pharmaceutical industry. Sixty-nine percent of the *DSM* task force had ties with big pharma. (57% of the *DSM IV* had such ties.) A petition was signed by 13,000 people and sponsored by various mental health organizations which called for outside review.

Psychiatry and Big Pharma have medicalized society in the name of politics and profit. They market directly to consumers for diseases that have no validity – for which there are no MRIs, no blood tests, or other evidence of their existence. Direct to consumer drug advertising tripled from 2000 to 2010 and from $1.3 billion in 1999 to $4.8 billion in 2008. In 1996, 13 million Americans took antidepressants. In 2005, this number rose to 27 million. One out of every ten Americans over the age of six are now taking an anti-depressant. And the use of sleeping pills has doubled from 2000 to 2004. In 2006, it was estimated that 8.6 million used these medications regularly.

In this context it would be counter-therapeutic to refer someone who is experiencing a spiritual crisis to a medical doctor — especially a psychiatrist. The result would be immediate medication and possibly hospitalization aimed at ending the crisis as quickly as possible. Far too many people have had their personal process interrupted by this sort of misdiagnosis, medication, and psychiatric treatment. The result is that the person in crisis is unable to complete the process and is left with a lifelong mental health label and shame from iatrogenic mistreatment.

Psychiatry has forgotten the essence of its mission — to treat the mind and has instead become obsessed with medications. But the truth is that mental illness is not a brain disorder. If it were then it would fall under the field of neurology. None of the explanations that have been floated have been proven. Serotonin deficiency has been proposed by working backward from the effect of medications but there is no evidence of serotonin deficiency. To offer such an explanation would be like positing a morphine deficiency based on the use of morphine to treat a heart attack. But the pain of a heart attack is not from lack of morphine; it's from a lack of oxygen to certain cardiac tissues. The true explanation was not guided by the development of cardiac medications but that is exactly how psychiatric explanations are developed.

The point is that psychiatry and to large extent psychology have failed to provide the understanding and healing which they originally pursued. They have been co-opted by psychopathology and pharmacology. They have disowned the psyche (the soul) as a legitimate aspect of their study. This failure can be seen in the increase of mental illness in America. Not surprisingly this failure has been noted by others. Tanya Luhrmann observes in *Of Two Minds: The Growing Disorder in American Psychiatry* that it is fashionable in some intellectual circles to deny the existence of mental illness (2000:10). Foucault (1967), R.D. Laing (1969), Thomas Szasz (1961) are among the prominent critics of psychopathology. They, in fact, argue that there are no behaviors which are inherently pathological. Part of the argument is that pathology, or normalcy for that matter, is to an extent defined by the cultural context. So, if people having spiritual experiences meet the world of psychiatry they risk being labeled mentally ill.

The failures of Western psychiatry in general highlight the futility of applying such approaches to the understanding of spiritual emergencies. Those interested in helping people who are experiencing such crises must leave aside the conventional world of psychodiagnosis. Applying such approaches is more likely to result in confusion, negative self-perceptions, and even medication for those experiencing spiritual crises. Such approaches are unlikely to result in integration or even understanding.

Sara E. Lewis addressed this issue in relationship to spiritual crisis:

> Although patients present with familiar symptoms ranging from depression to paranoid delusions, the etiology of the symptoms is unfamiliar territory.

This marks a slew of moral and ethical clinical issues. If the clinician's *own* religious beliefs prevent him or her from believing that the patient had a near-death experience or communicated with a dead relative, for example, the question remains if the clinician will provide optimal therapy. Among the clinicians I interviewed, there seems to be agreement that more training and sensitivity is needed in the profession (Lewis, 2008, P. 114).

While it is certainly true that clinicians need more training and sensitivity to spiritual events and world views, that is not enough. Training among therapists and other helpers will not be able to overcome the monolithic allopathic approach of psychiatry and the behemoth of Big Pharma. The underlying assumptions and motivations of these entities preclude any true understanding or useful intervention. My recommendation would be to those who are experiencing spiritual crises to avoid traditional, conventional practitioners. To therapists and other would-be helpers, I would urge a rigorous consideration of your values and assumptions.

For those interested in exploring the problems with the DSM there are a large number of publications including Edward Shorter's *How Everyone Became Depressed: The Rise and Fall of the Nervous Breakdown*, Gary Greenberg's *The Book of Woe: The DSM and the Unmaking of Psychiatry* and *Saving Normal: An Insider's Revolt Against Out-of-Control Psychiatric Diagnosis*.

The failure of psychiatry and psychology to prevent or to humanely treat mental illness is one of the worst failures of our society and will undoubtedly be seen so in the future. From a spiritual emergence perspective this failure is even greater since it involves ignoring and even suppressing the potential growth of individuals along with the insights they could have provided while experiencing their spiritual emergence. R.D. Laing, the great psychologist, said it eloquently in reference to schizophrenia:

> If the human race survives, future men will, I
> suspect, look back on our enlightened epoch
> as a veritable Age of Darkness. They will see that
> what   was considered 'schizophrenia' was one of
> the forms in which, often through quite ordinary
> people, the light began to break into our all too-
> closed minds. (Ronald D. Laing quoted in "So-
> called schizophrenia")

Chapter Four-Altered States of Consciousness

The study of altered states of consciousness, which are also known as non-ordinary states of consciousness, trance, mystical states, shamanic consciousness, and other names is an important aspect of modern Psychology and especially Transpersonal Psychology. It is, however, a dangerous field that has led some researchers to be discounted and some even to experience legal problems related to their research. To the materialistic fundamentalists who dominate the field of Psychiatry, altered states with their associated phenomena are not worthy of serious consideration. On the other hand, the study of such states has contributed significant insights into the nature of the human mind.

William James, the pioneer of so many aspects of consciousness studies, used nitrous oxide to explore its effects on the human mind and reached important insights concerning the continuum of consciousness. He wrote in his classic *Varieties of Religious Experience:*

> Some years ago I myself made some observations on this aspect of nitrous oxide intoxication, and repeated them in print. One conclusion was forced upon my mind at that time, and my impression of its truth has ever since remained unshaken. It is our normal waking consciousness, rational con-sciousness as we call it, is but one special type of consciousness, whilst all about it, parted from it by the filmiest of screens, there lie potential forms of

consciousness entirely different. We may go
through life without suspecting their existence,
but apply the requisite stimulus, and at a touch
they are there in all their completeness, definite
types of mentality which probably somewhere
have   their field of applications and adaptation.
No account of the universe in its totality can be
final which leaves these other forms of consciousness quite discarded. How to regard them is the
question, -- for they are discontinuous with
ordinary consciousness (James, 1902).

But these insights are not accepted by psychiatrists
in general and even most mental health professionals tend
to ignore them – if they know of them at all. Altered
states of consciousness are more often seen as aberrant,
anomalous, or even pathological. Yet it is hard to think of
any area of study that would be more central to the study
of psychology than that concerned with the nature of
consciousness. Nicki Crowley summarizes the two basic
approaches to the study of consciousness:

Medicine, psychiatry and traditional
psychotherapies hold the assumption that
consciousness is a by-product (or epiphenomenon)
of the brain and cannot persist independently of it
(the productive theory of consciousness). The
transmissive theory of consciousness holds that
consciousness is inherent in the cosmos and is
independent of our physical senses, although
is mediated by them in everyday life. So the brain
as the psyche can be thought of acting as a lens
through which consciousness is experienced in
the body. (Crowley, 2006, p. 2)

All too frequently the assumption is made that an
altered   state   of   consciousness   is   negative.   The

109

experiences of altered states are considered to be symptoms of some sort of dysfunction in the brain. They have been considered over the centuries to be the product of demonic interference or heathen practices that required exorcism, cleansing, repentance, or even violent defiance through crusades, inquisitions, or incarceration in prison or hospital. In modern times the War on Drugs has taken on many of the characteristics of both crusade and inquisition in its attempt to control how people control or alter their own consciousness.

But unfortunately for the opponents to altered states of consciousness, they persist and even prosper. This may be due in part to them being a universal aspect of being human. In fact they have frequently been used to treat psychological issues: The induction of these states has been employed for almost every conceivable aspect of psychological therapy" (Ludwig, 1969, p. 19). All cultures have some means of altering states of consciousness. These include drugs, plants, alcohol, rituals, isolation, running, breathing exercises, hypnosis, dancing, music, ordeals, and much more. They also include spontaneous mystical experiences. In the summer of 1881, Nietzsche experienced just such an experience during which he saw the *übermensch* – "he is the lightening, he is this madness".

These technologies persist (and even proliferate) because of the positive benefits they bring to individuals and societies. Stanislav Grof, a pioneer of LSD studies including Psychedelic Therapy and a founder of Transcendental Psychology, made this observation on the benefits of altered states of consciousness:

> There exist spontaneous non-ordinary states of consciousness, (NOSC) that would in the West be seen and treated as psychosis, and treated mostly

110

by suppressive medication. But if we use the observations from the study of non-ordinary states, and also from other spiritual traditions, they should really be treated as crises of transformation, or crises of spiritual opening.   Something that should really be supported rather than suppressed. If properly understood and properly supported, they are actually conducive   to healing and transformation (Grof and Redwood, 1995, pp. 1-2).

Abraham Maslow considered altered states of consciousness, which he called "peak experiences", to be a characteristic of the self-actualized person. Maslow went on to attribute social and religious impact to the altered states of individuals.   He believed that the origin and essence of "high religions" was "the private, lonely, personal illumination, revelation, or ecstasy of some acutely sensitive prophet or seer" (Maslow, 1970. In Sadler, 1970, p. 19). In his studies of peak experiences he mentions "mystic or oceanic experiences so profound as to remove neurotic symptoms forever after" (Maslow, A.H. *Genetic Psych.*, 94:45-66, 1959. Quoted in Sherwood, et al., p. 77).   Maslow criticized Western psychiatry for confusing mystical states with mental illness. Rather than considering such states to be abnormal he believed they should be considered supernormal (Maslow, 1964).

Altered States of Consciousness are among the most ancient healing traditions (Walsh, 1990; Eliade, 1974). Yet most approaches to modern therapy operate within ordinary consciousness or at least a presumption of ordinary consciousness.   Certain approaches probably induce altered states even if the therapist is unaware of it. The teachings of Milton Erickson, M.D. demonstrate that altered states play a much larger role in therapy than is

111

usually recognized (Erickson, 1980). Certain approaches, largely those influenced by Erickson, emphasize the role of altered states. In a personal conversation with the inspiring family therapist Virginia Satir she told me that she did not believe any change occurs in therapy without some sort of trance.

Metzner defines an altered state of consciousness as a change from one's ordinary consciousness in terms of thinking, feeling, and perception (Metzner, 1995). Shamans frame altered states as journeys to other realms where a person can gain information and insights then return to apply them in this reality (Kalweit, 1992). Religious conversions are also examples of changes in thinking, feeling and perceptions that occur in altered states of consciousness.

Resistance to the use of altered states of consciousness sometimes involves the belief that such states are temporary and superficial and that they do not contribute to lasting changes. But the evidence leads us to believe otherwise. People who have experienced ecstatic union frequently report long-term profound changes (Krishna, 1971; Krippner, Leibovitz, 1977). Studies of mystical experience also indicate improved psychological functioning and trait changes (Tart, 1990). There is a vast amount of evidence indicating long term changes with the use of hypnotherapy (Erickson and Rossi, 1981). Near Death Experiences (NDE) also produce significant changes in the personalities of those who experience them. They usually become more compassionate, more loving, and have a greater sense of meaning in life. In follow up studies at two and eight years researchers found a significant difference between patients with and without an NDE. The process of transformation took several years to consolidate. Patients with an NDE did not show any fear of death, they strongly believed in an afterlife, and their insight in what is important in life had changed: love and compassion for oneself, for others, and for nature.... Furthermore, the long lasting transformational effects of an experience that lasts only a few minutes was a surprising and unexpected finding (Van Lommel, 2004, p. 118).

Religious and spiritual approaches to altered states

There are numerous methods of inducing altered states of consciousness which are used by religions and spiritual disciplines. This is not surprising given that one purpose of religion is, as Eliade proposes, to create a sacred place that is different from the normal daily profane space. This space is essentially a matter of creating an altered state of consciousness. The methods of creating sacred space can be as ordinary as singing hymns, reciting creeds, and publicly praying. Other methods may be practiced in groups or individually. These include but are certainly not limited to meditating, yoga, fasting, walking a prayer circle, making a pilgrimage, taking sacraments, singing with a choir, participating in retreats, dancing, lighting candles, prayer, contemplating the sunrise, receiving baptism or *mikveh*, foot washings, weddings, hand-fastings, flower baths, and participating in sadhana.

Of course these rituals may serve other purposes such as serving as rites of passage and there are similar rituals that fall outside a strictly religious context that while serving a secular function can and often do result in altered states of consciousness. These include graduation ceremonies, awards ceremonies, inaugural ceremonies, and even such things as singing the national anthem and similar secular rituals. In this way secular rituals can share many aspects of religious ritual and draw us into an individual or collective altered state of consciousness.

These rituals may serve various purposes – building civic pride, patriotism, building political good will, rites of passage but it is clear that even the most secular ritual owes something to an ancient religious practice. Most of what we now consider secular was at one time religious. The oaths of politicians, robes of justices, choral celebrations, and much more originated with some ancient purpose – possibly even even prehistoric, religious practice. Both secular and religious ceremonies continue to have much in common.

What all of these practices have in common, however, is the way in which they integrate different aspects of our human experience – our emotions with our intellect or our minds with our bodies – while also connecting us with others who share similar beliefs. We seek out these experiences, which are special and set us distinctly apart from our mundane and ordinary daily lives. These experiences lift us up out of our narrow selves and give us a glimpse – if only temporary – of another way to view things as a part, however small, of a larger picture. Spiritual and religious practices that help us integrate the body, mind, and spirit, also provide psychological and physical benefits, as research from the past two decades has shown (Idler, 2008, p. 1)

Religion plays an important role in helping people in moving from one phase of life to the next. Many of these transitions are accompanied by rituals such as, baptism, confirmation, circumcision, and rites of passage and occur early in life. Others may indicate a change in social role or status or provide comfort.

Many religions provide rules and guidance on lifestyle issues such as diet, the use of substances, and behavior toward others. Wallace and Forman at the University of Michigan found that adolescents for whom religion plays an important role and who attend religious services frequently have lower rates of tobacco, alcohol and marijuana use, higher rates of seat belt use, and eat more nutritious foods. They have lower rates of carrying weapons, fighting, and driving while drinking (Wallace and Forman, 1998; Igler, p. 2). Such behaviors have long-term benefits on their health and well-being. Many other studies have reached similar conclusions (Strawbridge, et al., 1997; Berkman and Syme, 1979; House, Landis, and Umberson, 1988). Religious activities also contribute to more prosocial behaviors, greater social ties and a stronger feeling of support (Ellison and George, 1998).

Of course, religious practices offer altered states of consciousness as well. Emile Durkheim spoke about "sacred time" as distinguished from the "profane time" which comprises most of our daily lives. Such things as meditation, prayer, candle lighting, worship-service, quiet retreats, and rituals help set time off as sacred and special. These experiences also help to heal. And, these various activities and experiences seem to have a cumulative positive effect. Religious practices also have an intrinsic value beyond the healthy side effects. Spirituality and religion address matters of ultimate concern in the lives of people

Interestingly, a group of researchers determined that the experience of taking Psilocybin mushrooms equated to having a peak experience not only as a mystical experience but in terms of "having substantial and

115

sustained personal meaning and spiritual significance" (Griffiths, et al, 2008). Panke and Richards also compared LSD and mystical experiences with peak experiences. Their criteria for a peak experience could equally be applied to mystical experiences. They are unity (inner and outer), strong positive emotions, transcendence of time and space, a sense of sacredness (numinosity), paradoxical nature of the experience, objectivity and reality of the insights, ineffability, and positive after-effects (Panke & Richards, 1966).

Although frequently devalued and even demonized in modern Western society, altered states of consciousness have played a significant role in the development of human society and possibly even in the evolution of humanity. As seen above, Maslow considered them to have been a significant influence on religion and when we consider the role religion played in early society that increases the significance even more.

It is clear from anthropology, history, and even archaeology that societies throughout the world have developed techniques for altering consciousness. Shamanism is considered by many to be essentially a method for altering consciousness. Mircea Eliade titled his landmark study – *Shamanism: Archaic Techniques of Ecstasy.* The techniques of shamanism include sensory deprivation in caves, isolation through ordeals, physical ordeals like the Sun Dance, physical exhaustion, dance, singing, drumming, and of course the use of entheogens such as tobacco, cannabis, mushrooms, and ayahuasca, to name just a few. The anthropologist Michael Harner has placed emphasis on the use of drumming and what he calls sonic driving for achieving shamanic states of consciousness. Some shamanic traditions use intentional possession and mediumship.

The ethnobotanist Terence McKenna proposed that human evolution was aided by the use of hallucinogenic plants such as psilocybin mushrooms. In this theory, sometimes called the "Stoned Ape" theory, human ancestors invented culture and developed the mind after being altered by entheogens. Evidence of this is growing. In 1987 researchers in Tanzania's Mahale Mountains National Park observed an isolated female chimpanzee who was so sick she could barely move. They observed her dragging herself to a Veronia amygdaline bush where she tore off and chewed some of the foul tasting shoots for their juice and spit out the fibrous parts. By the following afternoon she was completely healed and was socializing with other chimpanzees. This may have been the first time scientists had observed a wild animal using medicinal plants for healing. It is interesting that the native people of the area use the same plant for parasites and gastrointestinal disorders (Marling, pp. 1-2). Animals seek out and use medicinal plants and they seek consciousness-altering plants as well.

Harvard anthropologist Richard Wrangham has observed a large number of chimpanzees walking for 20 minutes or more in search of Aspilia, a plant in the sunflower family. The animals gulp the leaves down whole even at times to the point of vomiting. It has been found since these observations that Aspilia is high in thiarubine-A, a red oil which kills parasites, fungi, and viruses. Biochemists have found that that the thiarubrine kills cancer cells in solid tumors. Further research has found that at least fifteen different species of medicinal plants are used by chimpanzees. These plants are used in a range from potions to salves for a number of different ailments (Marling, p. 2).

Further it is not just chimpanzees or even primates that use plants as medicine. There are so many animals who used plant medicines that a new branch of zoology has developed to study the phenomenon – zoopharmacognosty (Begley and Leonard, 1992). This new branch of science has discovered that animals use plants to deliberately alter their consciousness. In 1970, Ronald Siegel, a psychopharmacologist at the UCLA School of Medicine discovered a painting on a shard from an ancient bowl in Peru related to this issue. The painting represents two llamas eating coca leaves. It also shows two Indians pointing to the llamas while they are reaching for the leaves with open mouths. Siegel found that the incident portrayed on the pottery shard is not an isolated incident (Marling, p. 3). An Abyssinian legend from around 900 CE tells how a herder discovered coffee while watching his animals become energized by eating the berry. A similar story from Yemen tolls how a shepherd discovered *qat,* an hallucinogenic plant, after seeing his goats run while after eating certain leaves. In the mountains of Sikkim, tired horses regularly consume bitter tea leaves for energy. Pack donkeys in Mexico grazed on wild tobacco for the same reason. In Cambodia it was observed that free-ranging water buffalo and antelope increased their grazing of opium poppies possibly in response to stress from the wartime environment. In Africa, elephants eat the fermented fruit of doum and marula trees which can contain alcohol up to 7% and which have the same effect on elephants as that range of alcohol has on humans. In Columbia jaguars gnaw on the bark of yaje (also known as ayahuasaca). The indigenous people believe the jaguars fly to other worlds by doing this. In West Africa wild boars dig for the roots of the hallucinogenic plant iboga and they react to the plant with altered behavior. In the Asian tundra, reindeer eat the Amanita muscaria which is also used by Siberian shamans in their spiritual journeys (Siegal, 1989).

Given the widespread use of medicinal including mind-altering plants among animals and humans, it is likely that entheogens influenced development of culture (Rush, 2013). The evidence for this can be seen in ancient scriptures. The Hindu scripture known as the *Rg-Veda* has over a hundred hymns devoted to Soma which was a psychoactive substance which may have involved the Amanita Muscaria. The Zoroastrian scriptures mention the same or a similar substance called *homa* or *haoma*. The Greeks, who are often represented as the inventors of such Western concepts as democracy, the scientific method, literature, and medicine, are usually on closer examination the inheritors of older cultures including Sumer, Babylonia, Persia and even the greater Iranian world of the Scythians and other Iranian nomads as well as the advanced sedentary cultures found throughout Greater Iran. Not surprisingly they used entheogenic substances in the Mysteries of Eleusis and in other rituals. There is some evidence that the Eleusian mysteries involved the use of ergot, a precursor to LSD (Marling, p. 6). The mysteries and rituals of Dionysus were another "Greek" function that was introduced by Thracians, contained Indo-Iranian elements, and which involved the use of psychoactive substances

In the Americas there are numerous psychoactive plants which have been used medicinally and sacramentally. Among the best known of these is the Lophophora williamsii, or peyote cactus. Although originally confined to Northern Mexico and the southern U.S. border region, it is now widely used as a sacrament in the Native American Church. The Native Americans also used a number of other psychoactive plants including tobacco, ayahuasca, datura, the San Pedro cactus, and a variety of mushrooms just to name a few of the entheogenic plants that have been used in ceremonies to heal, gain power, or to get in touch with the spirit world.

Cannabis was used by the ancient Iranian nomads known as Scythians, and later by the Chinese, and the Indians. It was and is used by Sufis, Sadhus, Taoists, and Buddhists for religious purposes. Ancient Iranians had Haoma and the Indians had Soma. Then there are tobacco, mushrooms, datura, and many more including coffee and alcohol – not to mention hallucinogenic toads and toxic gases. Andrew Weil considers the use of drugs to be universal: "The ubiquity of drug use is so striking that it must represent a basic human appetite" (Weil, 1972).

Given the near universality of such plants as well as their widely touted benefits it is strange that we as a society are not more interested. But then we live in a perpetual War on Drugs which includes a war on any culture, behavior, or thought that lies too far outside the accepted ways approved by the dominant society. We are forced to wonder with Marling (2014, p. 11): "Isn't it strange that all we hear about is drug abuse, but nothing about drug use?:

Not only is the use of medicinal, entheogenic plants nearly universal but there is a certain mindset that goes with their use. This mindset involves an awareness of the connection of all things including people in Nature. It is a belief in the immanence of divinity. Among certain traditions this can be seen as pantheism. In others it might be seen as monism. But in any case it is an ancient tradition we can find among the ancient Greeks, in the teachings of philosophers like Johannes Scotus Erigena

(815-877), the German theologian Meister Eckhart, and the Sufi master Ibn al'Arabi.

Altered states have played an important role in discovery and intellectual development. Francis Crick, the discoverer of the double helix structure of DNA, was inspired by an experience with LSD. Many other inventors and important figures in modern technology have admitted to using LSD as part of their creative process. These include Douglas Englebart, the inventor of the computer mouse, Myron Stolaroff, a former Ampex engineer, and Steve Jobs, the co-founder of Apple. Then there are poets, writers, artists and so many others whose lives and contributions have been influenced by some sort of altered state of consciousness.

Of course there are many other ways of altering your state of consciousness in addition to entheogens or drugs. These include meditation, yoga, sleep deprivation, isolation, running, sensory deprivation just to name a few. The real issue is not access to the altered state but rather the outcome. This can be quite varied and depends on many factors. First there are the factors of set and setting. Then there are the personality variables and intentions of the person involved. Timothy Leary observed:

> You can work with 1,000 people and help every
> one of them change   their way of thinking and
> their way of acting, but there are no statistics
> like hits, runs, and errors to tabulate your score.
> The problem is that   half the people you help
> are going to get better jobs, and half of them
> are going to quit the jobs they have. Half of them
> may increase the   intimacy and closeness and
> meaning in their marriages, but the other
> half may leave their wives. Changing a person's
> psyche is one thing,   but measuring results in an

observable way is another thing (Leary, 1969, p. 32).

Chapter Five-Spiritual Emergencies

In the course of human life it is common for people to experience transformative events. Most of these events ultimately lead to growth and increased wisdom. At times they are so powerful that they overwhelm us and cause us to flounder or struggle with their lessons. We can call such an experience a "spiritual crisis" or a "spiritual emergency". The term "spiritual emergency" was coined by Stanislav and Christina Grof. They defined a spiritual emergency as a crisis that occurs when the process of growth and change becomes chaotic and overwhelming.

> Individuals experiencing such episodes may feel that their sense of identity is breaking down, that their old values no longer hold true, and that the very ground beneath their personal realities is radically shifting. In many cases, new realms of mystical and spiritual experience enter their lives suddenly and dramatically, resulting in fear and confusion. They may feel tremendous anxiety, have difficulty coping with their daily lives, jobs, and relationships, and may even fear for their own sanity. (Grof & Grof, 1989: back cover)

Spiritual emergencies are transformational crises rather than psychiatric disorders (Kalweit, 1989:78). Though the reactions can be extreme and include depression, dissociation, and issues usually labeled "psychotic" the etiology of the distress is spiritual or religious. This positive frame of the experience is important to avoid the negativity and denial of spirituality intrinsic with disease-focused Western medicine. As Sara Lewis commented:

In the West, psychological symptoms are treated as 'attacks' on the healthy mind, and things to rid oneself of as quickly as possible. The psychological distress associated with spiritual emergencies, however, may be an opportunity for deep healing and transformation (Lewis, p. 113).

Although the crisis may be triggered by either external events or internal spiritual practice, the actual crisis may develop more from the person's perspective of the experience and the availability of resources for integrating and understanding the experience. If the process is interrupted or if the person does not have the resources needed for integration then this might be the precipitant for the actual crisis. Marion Hubbard has commented on this aspect of spiritual emergence:

> If in highly sensitive individuals the process of spiritual emergence is blocked for any reason the person might be worried that their growth is in grave danger and that they rapidly need to make adjustments which are essential for effective adaptation. The transformation process of spiritual emergence can be so dramatic as to become uncontrollable and reach a point of crisis or emergency. So-called 'spiritual emergency' is known by many names such as transpersonal experience, transpersonal crisis, psycho-spiritual transformation, psycho-spiritual crisis, spiritual journey, hero's journey, dark night of the soul, spiritual opening, psychic opening, psychic awakening, spiritual awakening, enlightenment,

Kundalini awakening, Kundalini process, Kundalini crisis, shamanic initiation, shamanic crisis, psychotic-visionary episode, ego death, ego loss, alchemical process, positive disintegration, post traumatic stress disorder with psychotic features, night sea journey, psychosis, shamanism, mysticism, gnosis, inner apocalypse, and so on. (Hubbard, 2009, p. 3)

Sara Lewis further emphasizes the importance of avoiding the Western disease-focused approach when dealing with spiritual emergencies:

Stanislov and Christina Grof argue '[i]t is essential that [people dealing with spiritual emergencies] move away from the concept of disease and recognize the healing nature of their crisis' (1989:192). Many Western clinicians are not accustomed to treating their patients outside of a disease model and are thus not trained properly to work with patients coping with spiritual emergencies. In a survey of Association of Psychology Internship Centers training directors, '83 [percent] reported that discussions of religious and spiritual issues in training occurred rarely or never. One hundred percent indicated that they had received no education or training in religious or spiritual issues in clinical training' (cited in Lukoff 1998:22). (Lewis, P. 113)

Although it can be useful to categorize spiritual emergencies in order to develop individually and culturally sensitive approaches for intervention. It is important to avoid developing a taxonomy which is nothing more than a substitute for the disease-focused approach of Western psychiatry and psychology. Spiritual Emergencies can be difficult but they are not mental illnesses. Even within the context of the *Diagnostic and Statistical Manual* they are not viewed as mental disorders. As Lukoff notes, someone who is experiencing a spiritual emergency may "appear to have a mental disorder if viewed out of context, but are actually undergoing a 'normal reaction' which warrants a non-pathological diagnosis (i.e., a V Code for a condition not attributable to a mental disorder)" (Lukoff, 1998:23)

Rather than labeling a spiritual experience (whether emergence or emergency) as a mental illness it is much more useful to look on it as a fairly reasonable and natural consequence of dealing with transcendent and even Divine information. One researcher described it elegantly as "The uncontrollable influx of Divine material into one's life, creating psychological challenges as a result of a rapid growth of understanding" (Kane, 2005, p. 3).

William James with his usual profound insight proposed that judgment on spiritual experiences should be concerned with the results of such experiences rather than with some theoretical nosology or medical criteria. James wrote in *The Varieties of Religious Experience:* "To pass a spiritual judgment upon these states, we must not content ourselves with superficial medical talk, but inquire into their fruits for life" (James, 1902, p. 324).

Stanislav Grof has much to say about this subject. He coined the term "holotropic" to describe activities and states that are moving toward wholeness. He and his wife also coined the terms "spiritual emergence" and "spiritual emergency" as a partial play on words to indicate that such experiences play a role in the emergence of greater understanding and wholeness but that they can also be difficult. As one of the founders of Transpersonal Psychology, he has placed emphasis on the importance of spiritual values and experience. Concerning psychiatric diagnosis he wrote:

One of the most important implications of the research of holotropic states is the realization that many of the conditions, which are currently diagnosed as psychotic and indiscriminately treated by suppressive medication, are actually different stages of a radical personality trans-formation and of spiritual opening. If they are correctly understood and supported, these psychospiritual crises can result in emotional and psychosomatic healing, remarkable psychological transformation, and consciousness evolution....
(Grof. 2009)

The Spiritual Emergence Network (SEN) was founded in 1980 by Christina Grof at the Esalen Institute. In 1998 it was moved to the California Institute of Integral Studies. Over the years it has provided crisis intervention and support to many people experiencing spiritual emergencies. In the course it has developed protocols and understanding that have enabled them to provide more effective assistance to those who are undergoing such a crisis. In an interview, Karen Trueheart, the Director of SEN has emphasized the minimal role that labels of any sort play in helping with spiritual emergencies:

Categorization of experiences is not a main concern of the support staff at the Spiritual Emergence Network. Karen said that it's more important to be open to what people are saying and experiencing, and to help support the process, rather than giving experiences a label. The job of the staff is to listen and to accept the language that each person uses to describe his or her experience.

Some people call and say that they are in a Kundalini process. Someone else may call and say they are having a shamanic journey. Another person might say 'I am experiencing a dark night of the soul" Karen said. Two types of categories are used, however they are 'spontaneous' and intentional spiritual experience. (Adams, 2001)

Brother David Steindl-Rast, a Benedictine monk, has defined Spiritual Emergence as follows:

Spiritual emergence is a kind of birth pang in which you yourself go through to a fuller life, a deeper life, in which some areas in your life that were not yet encompassed by this fullness of life are now integrated or called to be integrated or challenged to be integrated. (Quoted in Bradgon, 1993, p. 18)

Nevertheless because of their academic training and the settings in which they work, many mental health professionals feel compelled to classify everything in the traditional insurance-dominated, disease-focused context of psychiatric diagnosis. As Stanislav Grof has observed:

Many mental health professionals who encounter the concept of psycho-spiritual crisis want to know the exact criteria by which one can make the 'differential diagnosis' between a crisis of this kind ('spiritual emergency') and psychosis.

Unfortunately, it is in principle impossible to make such differentiation according to the standards used in somatic medicine. Unlike disease treated by somatic medicine, psychotic states that are not obviously organic in nature – 'functional psychoses' or 'endogenous' psychoses are not medically defined. The commonly used laboratory examinations of blood, urine, stool, and cerebrospinal fluid, as well as EEG, X-rays, and other similar methods do not yield any useful clues in this regard. It is actually highly questionable whether these conditions should be called diseases at all. (Groff, 2009, p. 6)

Stan and Christina Grof developed a list of the varieties of psychospiritual crises. While this is not necessarily a comprehensive list, it is a useful place to start. The Grof's original eight were loss, questioning or change of spiritual values, mystical or unitive experience, psychic opening, kundalini, possession states, shamanistic crisis, UFO abduction, near-death experience, dying, grief and life-threatening illness. The Spiritual Emergency Network typology contains loss or change of faith, existential or spiritual crisis, experience of unitive consciousness or altered states, psychic openings, possession, near-death experience, kundalini, shamanic journey, and difficulties with meditation practice. Another early list made by the Grofs consisted of eleven items: shamanic experience, awakening of Kundalini, episodes of unitive consciousness such as mystical experiences and Maslow's "peak experience", psychological renewal, crisis of psychic opening including non-ordinary experiences and mediumistic channeling, past-life experiences, communication with spirit guides and channeling, near-death experiences (NDEs), close encounters with UFOs and alien abduction, possession states, and alcoholism and drug addiction which can be seen as a craving for transcendence or a sense of something missing in life.

Lukoff, Lu, and Turner (1998) provided an expanded list of twenty-three categories of spiritual emergencies that includes such items as joining a new faith, loss of faith, questioning spiritual values, and meditation-related problems. Mid-life crisis is seen by some as a spiritual crisis involving regression in the service of transcendence (Nelson, 1990; Washburn, 1988). The

129

Spiritual Emergence Network has identified "guru attack", the death and dying process and addictions as additional spiritual issues.

Clearly these categories have much to do with the specific context and experience of those involved. Although they may share certain experiences during the crisis itself, they are also highly dependent upon the individual's level of spiritual development, spiritual-religious background, family and social context and support. They are certainly useful in creating a framework for understanding the individual's experience but need not be perceived as diagnostic categories nor even understood as discrete categories. The list used here is taken from the Grofs' but should not be considered as comprehensive or as diagnostic.

1. Kundalini awakening
2. Shamanic crisis
3. Episodes of unitive consciousness (peak experiences)
4. Psychological renewal through return to the center
5. Psychic opening
6. Past-life experiences
7. Communications with spirit guides and channeling
8. Near-death experiences
9. Experiences of close encounters with UFOs
10. Possession states

It might be possible to develop a nosology based on the characteristics of the various types of Spiritual Emergency; however, the degree of overlap is so great that such an analysis is beyond the scope of this work. Elsewhere Grof has commented on the difficulty of developing discrete categories of spiritual emergencies: "It is difficult to categorize spiritual emergencies since each individual psyche is a multidimensional and multilevel system with no boundaries" (Grof, 2013). So rather than classify spiritual emergencies by their characteristics most writers in this area tend to classify them by their triggers – the events that precipitate the emergency.

Additionally, it may be that spiritual emergencies or spiritual emergence may play a much greater role in human affairs than is usually supposed. Perhaps some of the so-called mental illnesses are actually aspects of spiritual emergence. When considered more holistically perhaps we could conclude that there is a spiritual component to depression, anxiety, and even psychosis. Such an approach would certainly be more useful for professional helpers and would certainly be more valid than a reductionistic, materialist view that omits or ignores not just the spiritual but even the mental aspect of what it means to be human.

Precipitants

Many spiritual emergencies are triggered by active spiritual practices that are intended to bring about greater spirituality or spiritual emergence. These could include such things as prayer, reading the scripture, attendance at worship services, meditation, and other religious activities. But they could also involve shamanic activities, ceremonial magic, rituals such as baptism and marriage; or activities such as yoga and tai chi or even the use of entheogens such as ayahuasca, psilocybin mushrooms, and peyote.

Others might occur spontaneously in response to developmental events, regular life events, or unexpected events. These could include developmental issues involving physical maturation, social roles, and changes in one's relationships. They could involve relatively normal and expected events such as the natural deaths of loved ones, or unexpected events such as the loss of a job, an accident, major incidents, or trauma.

Spontaneous spiritual experiences and emergencies sometimes occur at unexpected moments when in the presence of natural phenomena. Of course these fall on a spectrum as do most human experience. It could range from the mere appreciation of a sunset to a full-blown mystical experience that transcends the mundane. Such spontaneous experiences occur among poets as is evident by their own reports. Gerard Manley Hopkins, Walt Whitman, D.H. Lawrence, William Blake and many other great poets have described the transcendent experience that at times comes with contemplating nature. But these experiences seem to occur among others as well. Moses was tending sheep when he came upon the burning bush. William Butler Yeats provided an elegant description of such an experience:

> My fiftieth year had come and gone
> I sat, a solitary man,
> In a crowded London shop,
> An open book and empty shop
> On the marble table-top,
>
> While on the shop and street I gazed
> My body for a moment blazed,
> And twenty minutes, more or less
> It seemed, so great my happiness,
> That I was blessed, and could bless.

Spiritual emergence and emergency can also result from threats to one's life in serious illness, accidents, or with medical operations. There is a significant body of literature that considers such experiences among mountaineers and other solitary adventurers. There is even a term for the experience of an unseen presence that provides comfort and support – the Third Man Factor or the Third Man Syndrome. The term can be traced to Sir Ernest Shackleton's book, *South*, in which he describes an unseen being helping him and two others to survive a thirty-six hour march on a glacier in Antarctica. This report inspired the poet, T.S. Eliot to include the following lines in his poem, *The Waste Land*:

> Who is the third who walks always beside you?
> When I count, there are only you and I together
> But when I look ahead up the white road
> There is always another one walking beside you
> Gliding wrapt in a brown mantle, hooded
> I do not know whether a man or a woman
> But who is that on the other side of you?

Others have also reported this experience including the mountaineers – Reinhold Messner, Peter Hillary, and Ann Bancroft. Shipwrecked men and solo sailors have also reported the experience as did Joshua Slocum who experienced a lengthy dialogue with one of Columbus's pilots. Charles Lindbergh reported it from his solo transatlantic flight.

Other things that can and have precipitated spontaneous spiritual experiences include dancing, listening to music, and sex. They can be experienced on awakening and even during certain sports like running. Other triggers can include:

1. Threats to life (serious illness, accidents, operations)
2. Extreme physical exertion, or prolong lack of sleep
3. Perinatal events (childbirth, miscarriage, abortion)
4. Powerful sexual experiences
5. Powerful emotional experiences (loss of close relationship)
6. Series of life failures
7. Deep involvement in various forms of meditation or other spiritual practices (most common)

In other words, a spiritual emergence or emergency does not necessarily depend upon a spiritual context or trigger. From a holistic approach this is not surprising. If we accept that the spirit, mind, and body are all parts of a united whole then we must see that an action in one part of the unit impacts the entire system. Our work impacts our family life. Our sexuality impacts our emotional and physical health. Our nutrition impacts our spirituality, and so on.

Spiritual emergence and emergencies occur in a context. We cannot divorce ourselves of social mores, morals, and beliefs. We might disown some of them but they still form part of our worldview. As evidence of this notice how disaffected members of churches or religions are often the most passionate enemies of their former belief. Even though they have left the church they define themselves in terms of the church. Just think of the many "recovering Catholics" you have met. Even more dramatic are the anti-Mormons who continue to center their lives on the Mormon Church even while denouncing it.

Disasters, wars, and other extreme experiences can also trigger spiritual emergence or emergency. Others have commented on how the best of humanity is often drawn out by the worst of circumstances. In extreme situations we often see heroism, altruism, compassion, cooperation, and other virtues which are not as apparent in ordinary daily life. We even see at times a surge of religious feeling and transcendence. Lukoff (2007) has observed that social change can also act as a trigger:

> Such visionary experiences are more likely to occur in societies undergoing rapid and devastating social change, such as with the Iroquois Indian leader Handsome Lake. In the late 1700s, he spent 6 months in a state of catatonia accompanied by visions. Following these experiences, he underwent a personal transformation, communicated his visions and new insights to others, and synthesized old and new beliefs into a new religion and way of living that revitalized the culture (p. 635).

There has even been some recognition for the fact that a spiritual emergency can lead to growth. As Lukoff (2007) has noted: "Several diagnostic categories have been proposed for such psychotic-like episodes which have potential for positive outcomes: problem-solving schizophrenia, positive disintegration, creative illness, spiritual emergencies, mystical experience with psychotic features, metanoiac voyages, and visionary states" (p. 635).

Other specific triggers might include certain spiritual practices such as Zen, Vipassana, Vajrayana Buddhist meditation, yoga, Sufi-practices, monastic contemplation, Christian prayer – to name a few. Such crises may be preceded by other factors which might include sleep deprivation, hunger, isolation, and other stressors. They are most likely to occur in societies which are undergoing rapid social change (Lukoff, 2007, p. 635).

Receiving a Reiki attunement involves receiving an energy healing treatment from a Reiki master which is performed to open up the channels of energy and facilitate healing by the person receiving the attunement. Although it is a benign process it has been known to trigger an emergence or emergency for some. Some people begin to experience strong emotions and psychic experiences after receiving a Reiki attunement. The helper will provide acceptance, support, and information to help people experiencing such a crisis to integrate these new feelings and skills into life and hopefully into their practice as Reiki practitioners.

Another contributor to spiritual emergencies in modern Western society is a lack of preparation and the lack of a supportive context for many. The modern world with its increased mobility and greatly increased access to information has made formerly esoteric – even secret – knowledge and practices available and even familiar to people around the world. In centuries past only initiates were familiar with practices such as Tai Chi, Kundalini yoga, and shamanism. Now these and other practices are commonly known of and readily accessible through the internet or from direct instruction in medium to large-sized cities throughout the United States. They are available but without the social context of support and at times possibly too available to people who do not have a social or cultural context to support their practice. Initiations, after all, have often been more a matter of preparation than of secrecy. Mariana Caplan has commented on this factor in her *Halfway Up the Mountain: The Error of Premature Claims of Enlightenment*:

> Whereas spiritual masters have been warning their
> disciples for   thousands of years about the

dangers of playing with mystical states, the contemporary spiritual scene is like a candy store where any casual spiritual 'tourist' can sample the 'goodies' that promise a variety of mystical highs. When novices who don't have the proper education or guidance begin to naively and carelessly engage mythical experiences, they are playing with fire. Danger exists on the physical and psychological levels, as well as on the level of one's continued spiritual development" (Caplan, 1999).

Although some people who experience a spiritual crisis will seek medical treatment for their anxiety or other symptoms, efforts should be made to avoid giving them a *DSM* diagnosis. Lukoff argues for the use of the lesser non-pathological label of Religious or Spiritual Problem which is V62.89 in the *DSM V*. Lukoff says a person experiencing a spiritual crisis may

appear to have a mental disorder if viewed out of context, but are actually undergoing a 'normal reaction' which warrants a non-pathological diagnoses (i.e., a V Code for a condition not attributable to a mental disorder)." (Lukoff 1998:23)

This non-pathological V-code first appeared in the *DSM-IV* because of the efforts of Transpersonal psychologists. The *DSM V* retains it as one of the "Other Conditions That May Be a Focus of Clinical Attention" and states clearly, "The conditions and problems listed in this chapter are not mental disorders" (DSM V, p. 715). Examples of Religious or Spiritual Problems include loss or questioning of faith, problems associated with conversion to a new faith, and questioning spiritual values not necessarily related to an organized church or religious institution. While this is certainly a laudable improvement it is little more than a token recognition of spiritual issues. In everyday practice it is unusual for a mental health professional to use this code. For one thing most of the field is driven by the need to receive reimbursement from insurance companies who generally limit payment to the most familiar Axis I diagnoses and will often not reimburse at all for V codes (after all they are not technically mental disorders). Pharmaceutical companies also encourage the mental health field to focus on medical diagnoses that can be treated with drugs. Acknowledging spiritual issues detracts from the pharmaceutical approach. And, as mentioned elsewhere many mental health professionals share the materialistic biases of psychiatry. Nevertheless it is a step, however small, in the right direction.

Not surprisingly mainstream psychiatry interprets the reports of visions and mystical experiences as evidence of mental illness although there is no adequate medical evidence to support such an assessment. Psychiatric literature is replete with articles and books that discuss the most appropriate diagnoses for historical figures known for spiritual experiences. St. John of the Cross has been called a "hereditary degenerate," Mohammad an epileptic, and St. Teresa of Avila an hysterical psychotic. Jesus, Buddha, Ramakrishna, and Sri Ramana Maharishi have all been labeled psychotic.

The concept of spiritual emergency has been influenced by anthropologists such as Arnold van Gennup and the study of *rites de passage*. The anthropologist, Victor Turner, used the concept of liminality in *The Forest of Symbols: Aspects of Ndembu Ritual* (1967) where he views rites of passage as markers between states (legal status, professional calling, social role, states of maturation). These rites of passage are marked by three phases: separation, liminality, and reaggregation. Separation is detachment from the previous state which was marked by social structure and expectations. Once detached the individual lives in an ambiguous state between the former state and future state with their clear understandable roles and expectations.

The term liminal derives from the Latin word *limen* which means threshold. The liminal state is marked by anxiety, discomfort, pain, and even altered states of consciousness. The person is in a state of reflection and "divested of previous habits of thought, feeling and action" (Turner 1967:105). Finally in the reaggregation phase, the identity is reshaped.

The liminal phase creates a state of vulnerability where familiar norms, values, and behaviors are no longer workable. "They are also divested of their previous habits of thought, feeling, and action" (Turner 1967:105). Turner also refers to this phase as a "stage of reflection" (Turner 1967:105). During this state the individual may express distress which can include discomfort, pain, or altered states of consciousness (Douglas 1966; Turner 1967).

Resolution of the spiritual crisis occurs when a person is able to move beyond the liminality phase into the reaggregation phase. New values, behaviors, and roles are adopted and the individual assumes a new status as a result of the initiation.

If we apply the initiation model to spiritual emergencies we still have the trigger which marks a break from past understandings, perceptions, and expectations. This is followed by the liminal phase during which the person finds that previous beliefs, values, behaviors, roles et cetera no longer apply to their experience. Eventually the crisis is resolved as the person integrates the new understanding into a new approach to life with new values and behaviors.

In the world of crisis management there are a number of models of crisis. Most of them have multiple steps and extend over many weeks. The approach with liminality has the advantage of being simple and is particularly applicable to a spiritual emergency. It should be noted though that positive resolution of a crisis is not a given. The person could move back down to the initial level in which they began or they could move down to a similar level without any significant integration of the new experience. The liminal phase could last an extended time and could possibly lead to deterioration or to resolution in a less functional level. Ideally, either with or without support, the crisis will resolve with integration of the experience and acquisition of new skills, values, behaviors, and roles.

Chapter Six-Pathways to Emergence and Triggers for Emergencies

A spiritual emergence can be thought of as a personal awakening which is beyond the normal functioning. Such an emergence could include an out-of-body-experience (OOBE), occult phenomena, pre-cognitive clairvoyance, astral travel, perception of auras, unitive consciousness, increased creativity, increased compassion, and non-ordinary states of consciousness. To someone who has not experienced a spiritual emergence it might look like psychopathology and in fact each of these experiences has been labeled as pathology at some point. The out-of-body-experience, for instance, which is fairly common with near death experiences used to be called "ICU psychosis". This is especially so if the person and those around her have no conceptual framework for such an experience.

The tendency to treat these experiences as psychopathology is increased when there is little or no physical or emotional flexibility. The person may also experience changes in body temperature, confusion, headaches (either pressure or tingling in the head), psychological upset, stress, depression; derealization, mood swings, hallucinations, or increased energy. However none of these – individually or collectively -- necessarily indicate pathology. They are all known to accompany the process of spiritual emergence. Confusion, for example, was commented on by Roberto Assagioli: Instances of such confusion are not uncommon among people who became dazzled by contact with truths too great or energies too powerful for their mental capacities to grasp and their personality to assimilate (Assagioli, 1989, p. 36).

The risk of a spiritual emergence turning into a spiritual emergency is increased if the person involved has little or no experience with spiritual issues and so no context or resources for understanding or dealing with non-ordinary states of consciousness. What is familiar or even expected in one culture might be completely foreign in another and so even more confusing or even threatening.

There is a potential risk of working with this type of energy – especially for beginners who are not familiar with it. Chögyam Trungpa said: "I will say that for beginners, it is extremely dangerous to play with energy, but for advanced students such work becomes relevant naturally (Trungpa, C., 1973, p. 74). This risk is heightened when these technologies are removed from a context where they are understood and where there are experienced guides and teachers to assist in the process.

> Traditionally, spiritual teachers have warned their students of the dangers and possible side effects of meditative techniques and help practitioners deal with these difficulties as they arose. Now that meditation is being marketed as a mass commodity, the information concerning the dangers and the necessary help is often not part of the package. Moreover, certain body therapies and human potential techniques appear to be triggering off the Kundalini syndrome completely outside the context of spiritual training and often the therapists themselves have no idea what this energy is, let alone how to deal with it (Kundalini Casualities, 1978, p. 47).

These statements are not meant to imply that such spiritual emergencies are only experienced in the West. They are a natural and human experience and have been known in all cultures and in all times. The potential for spiritual emergence carries with it the potential that the process can go awry. Even if the process proceeds as intended the extreme experience can still include a crisis period due to the extreme sessions and the huge adjustment involved.

The famous nineteenth-century Indian mystic Ramakrishna became insane while a priest of Kali and at other times demons disturbed him while he was meditating in a "Divine delirium" (Gupta, p. 405). He taught that the truly enlightened often acts mad. Romain Rolland wrote of experiences in his biography of Ramakrishna:

> He was no longer capable of performing the temple rites. In the midst of the ritual acts he was seized with fits of unconsciousness, sudden collapses and petrifactions, when he lost the control of the use of his joints and stiffened into a statue....
> Minute drops of blood oozed through his skin. His whole body seemed on fire... He became the Gods himself.... He was the great monkey, Hanuman (Rolland, 1979, pp. 36-37).
>
> The legion of Gods swooped upon him like a whirlwind. He was torn in pieces. He was divided against himself. His madness returned tenfold. He saw demonic creatures emerging from him.... He remained motionless, watching these manifestations issue from him.... He felt madness approaching.... Two years went by in this orgy of

mental intoxication and despair (Rolland, 1979, p 41).

Similar conditions can arise from occult practices such as ceremonial magic (Conway, 1973, pp. 129-132). Even a basic practice such as the Lesser Banishing Ritual of the Pentagram or the Middle Pillar Ritual when practiced regularly and diligently can result in some startling experiences for the would-be mage.

Kundalini

Kundalini awakening is the most frequently reported form of spiritual emergency. Kundalini Yoga which is sometimes called Laya Yoga is a powerful technology for generating energy and along with it spiritual experiences and altered states of consciousness. The aim is to generate energy for healing and helping others. The name can mean "circular", "serpent" or "serpent-like" and alludes to the Kundalini energy which is said to lie coiled like a snake at the base of the spine.

Kundalini is a form of Tantric Yoga which is an approach to meditation and ritual. It is mentioned in the seventeenth century *Yoga Kundalini Upanishad* but it is closely related to Hatha Yoga. Swami Nigamanda, who died in 1935, taught a form of Kundalini Yoga and insisted that it is not Hatha but rather a part of Laya Yoga. In 1935 Swami Sivananda Saraswati wrote that Kundalini is not part of Hatha Yoga. But the most important figure in Kundalini Yoga, at least in the West, is Yogi Bhajan who introduced Kundalini in America in 1968 as part of the Sikh Dharma. Yogi Bhajan taught that Kundalini was part of Raj Yoga.

A Kundalini Awakening can involve the feeling of energy in the spine, tremors, shaking, spasms, complex twisting movements, visions of lights, involuntary vocalizations, crying, and auditory phenomena along with emotional and psychological upheaval. As a Kundalini Yoga Instructor I have frequently witnessed spontaneous laughter or crying even in a routine yoga class. Stanislav Grof describes it as follows:

> During Kundalini experiences such as this, the person may begin laughing or crying involuntarily. They may start chanting songs or mantras, speaking in tongues, emitting animal sounds, and assuming spontaneous yogic gestures and postures. To the uninitiated observer the person having such an experience may appear to have completely lost their senses. And for the person undergoing the experience without proper preparation, there may be fear that they are going crazy. However, when one approaches the Kundalini experience within the yogic tradition it is seen as an increased awareness of what we call the transpersonal realm, and a dramatic opening to spiritual life. (Grof, 1990, pp. 147-148)

Not surprisingly this powerful technology also at times generates spiritual emergencies which are sometimes referred to as Kundalini Emergencies. Other names for this type of spiritual emergency include Qi Gong Deviation Syndrome which is a diagnosis used in China, and which is alluded to as qi gong psychotic disorder and mentioned as such in the *DSM-IV* in Appendix I. There are also qigong psychosis, evil qi (*xie qi*), malignant qi, stagnant qi, and Kundalini syndrome which have collectively been referred to as the dark side of qi. This emergency occurs of course with the practice of yoga and meditation but also with disciplines that focus on qi such as Taiqi, Reiki, and Aikido. The newsletter for the Spiritual Emergency Network reported that 24% of their hotline calls concerned Kundalini awakening (Lukoff, 1988).

The symptoms of such an emergency can include disorientation, disconnect with reality, psychotic-like symptoms, sleep disruption, and decreased appetite. Intervention includes grounding by doing certain yogic exercises including breathing exercises or pranayama as well as more directly grounding by doing such things as walking barefoot outside. These emergencies are said to result from moving too much prana up but can also be triggered by traumatic life experiences. As a Kundalini instructor I was taught by Mehtab at Yoga Yoga in Austin, Texas that the intervention for pranic imbalances (another name for a Kundalini Emergency) was to use pranayama as follows:

1. Breath long and deep through left nostril for 3 to 5 minutes
2. Breath long and deep through right nostril for 3 to 5 minutes
3. Inhale through left nostril, exhale through right nostril for 3 to 5 minutes
4. Inhale through right nostril, exhale through left nostril for 3 to 5 minutes
5. Sitali pranayama; breath thru extended curled tongue for 3 to 5 minutes.
6. Breath of Fire for 3 to 5 minutes.
7. Long deep breathing with hands clasped in front of chest for 3 to 5 minutes.
8. Sat Kriya for 3 to 5 minutes.
9. Sa Ta Na Ma Meditation for eleven minutes.
10. Repeat steps 8 and 9 if needed or possible.

11. Deep relaxation for 30 minutes to music with the Guru Ram Dam mantra.

This series is to be practiced for forty days ideally working up to 5 minutes for steps 1 through 8. Step 9, the Sa Ta Na Ma Meditation, is to be repeated as follows: 2 minutes out loud, 2 minutes whispered, 3 minutes silent, 2 minutes, two minutes whispered, and 2 minutes out loud.

There are other kriya and meditations available as well. Another intervention that is sometimes suggested is to place a cup of water where negative energy manifests and then to check the water after a couple of hours. If bubbles are present then it is said that the negative energy is being absorbed. The water can be thrown out and replaced if needed.

An additional approach that can be useful with a Kundalini experience and other forms of spiritual emergency is the technique of mindfulness. Although mindfulness is usually considered to be a Buddhist technique, it can be found in many traditions including Sufism and Christianity. Essentially it involves a process of grounding by bringing attention to the body, sensations, and the immediate surroundings and activities. Following is an example of the use of mindfulness with a spiritual emergency as described by Jack Kornfield:

An 'overzealous young karate student' decided to meditate and not move for a full day and night. When he got up, he was filled with explosive energy. He strode into the middle of the dining hall filled with 100 silent retreatants and began to yell and practice his karate maneuvers at triple speed. Then he screamed, 'When I look at each of you, I see behind you a whole trail of bodies showing your past lives.' As an experienced meditation teacher, Kornfield recognized that the symptoms were related to the meditation practice rather than signs of a manic episode (for which they also meet all the diagnostic criteria except duration). The meditation community handled the situation by stopping his meditation practice and started him jogging, ten miles in the morning and afternoon. His diet was changed to include red meat, which is thought to have a grounding effect. They got him to take frequent hot baths and showers, and to dig in the garden. One person was with him all the time. After three days, he was able to sleep again and was allowed to start meditating again, slowly and carefully (Kornfield, 1989, pp. 131-132).

Uncomfortable sensations during a Kundalini awakening or other spiritual emergence can also be helped by attending to physical sensations by purifying the body. Steps that can help include abstaining from recreational drugs, tobacco, alcohol, caffeine, prescription drugs, food additives, refined sugar, and greasy foods. Massages and exercises will also help. Reduce your activities and stress. Find support from someone who has knowledge of this type of experience. Continue learning but not just intellectually. Allow yourself time for reflection and meditation. Reiki can also help to make the process less uncomfortable.

Meditation

Not all "Kundalini" experiences result from a Kundalini practice. There are many types of meditation and meditation is used as a tool in various religious and spiritual practices. These too could result in a spiritual emergency – even a Kundalini experience. A short list of such practices would include Zen, mindfulness, compassion meditation, Transcendental Meditation, Vipassana, and yoga just to name a few. And though to many Westerners, meditation is thought of as an Eastern practice, it is also firmly rooted in Christian practice.

Meditation can trigger a spiritual emergency. Tibetan Buddhists, who are among the most accomplished and informed meditators, report *soKrlung* which consists of awful visions, other altered perceptions, and an obsessive mindfulness that can result from meditation (Epstein, 1990). Some researchers have reported acute psychotic episodes precipitated by intensive meditation by individuals with a history of schizophrenia (Walsh and Roche, 1979). These episodes include changes that can be perceived as anxiety, dissociation, depersonalization, altered perceptions, and agitation by Western practitioners. However, Walsh and Roche (1979) point out that "...such changes are not necessarily pathologic and may reflect in part a heightened sensitivity" (p. 1086). Others have advocated for the use of meditation in psychotherapy (Bogart, 1991).

Father Thomas Keating started the Christian Century Prayer movement in the 1970s as part of Contemplative Outreach. This movement was influenced by the Desert Fathers and Mothers, The Cloud of Unknowing, St. John of the Cross, St. Teresa of Avila including, of course, St. Ignatius of Loyola, the founder of the Jesuits. In many ways it is a hearkening back to much older Christian traditions.

In Eastern Orthodox churches this is reflected in the Hesychasm which involves the repetition of the Jesus Prayer: Lord Jesus Christ, have mercy on me, the sinner. It is also found in the use of the Rosary. To those who follow a contemplative path this is based in the Biblical teaching of "constant prayer" and "meditation" is mentioned numerous times in the Bible. The Western Church also has the tradition of *Lectio divina* which involves the reading of Biblical passages followed by meditation on those passages.

Although these various forms of meditation are firmly grounded in the practices of the Primitive Church and the teachings of the Early Church Fathers as well as in the Bible, it would be naïve to expect them to be universally accepted. Evangelical and Fundamentalist Christians often criticize these practices. Some see them as a mixing of traditions – meaning Christian with Eastern religions. Others see them as an attack or distraction from Christ-centeredness. In any case, those who are seeking to provide guidance or help to Christians must be sensitive to differences in belief concerning both orthodoxy and orthopraxy. As much as possible effort must be taken to help people within their own belief system.

Mindfulness meditation is a practice based in Buddhist teachings which was brought to attention in the West largely though the teaching of Thich Nhat Hanh. Jon Kabat Zinn adopted the approach from Thich Nhat Hanh and applied it to the treatment of medical conditions. Others including Jack Kornfield, Joseph Goldstein, Tara Brach, and Marsha Linehan have played a role in popularizing mindfulness meditation. Additionally it has been incorporated in a number of therapeutic approaches. Gestalt therapy has been using it under the name of "awareness" since the early 1940s. Morita therapy is a Buddhist-based approach in Japan that uses mindfulness and non-attachment. Kabat-Zinn developed Mindfulness-Based Stress Reduction, Ron Kurtz and others developed Hakomi, a somatic approach which uses mindfulness, Mindfulness-based cognitive therapy (MBCT) applies mindfulness to psychological disorders. And Marsha Linehan's Dialectal Behavior Therapy (DBT) applies mindfulness to borderline personality disorder.

Mindfulness can be a useful approach to meditation and for helping someone to ground after a spiritual emergency. It is a useful spiritual discipline for anyone interested in developing an awareness of the Divine or in integrating spiritual experiences. Although often dominated by those who have learned from a Buddhist perspective, the practice is well-known in the history of other religions such as Christianity as mentioned above. It is sometimes known in the West as the practice of the presence.

Shamanic Crisis

A shamanic crisis involves a non-ordinary state of consciousness, also known as shamanic consciousness which traditionally has often been experienced concurrently with a life threatening illness, trauma or shamanic initiation. The emphasis on such an initiation has often been on suffering, an encounter with death, rebirth, and ascent. Such an experience may also involve power animals or totems, demons, a descent to the underworld, and an ascent to the upper world.

Lukoff (1991) has described the "shamanistic initiatory crisis" as a particular type of spiritual emergency which occurs when a non-shaman has spiritual experiences which occur more often in shamanic activities. These can include increased psychic ability, the ability to diagnose illness intuitively, communicating with spirits, and out-of-body traveling. When such experiences occur with non-Amazonian people during an ayahuasca ceremony they may trigger a spiritual crisis due to a lack of context or social support. Of course, they do not necessarily trigger a crisis since there are many non-Amazonians who accept such anomalous experiences. But some may experience some distress, feelings of isolation, or concern about what they experience.

From a shamanic perspective such a crisis is often part of the process of becoming a healer. It is a good thing and the correct response is to help the healer to be born. It results from the merging and development of energy and problems result when the person does not receive the needed help in dealing with the unfamiliar higher energy.

Malidoma Patrice Somé, a Dagara shaman from Africa, came to the United States in 1980 for graduate school. His response to our mental health system is revealing. Concerning his first visit to a psychiatric facility Dr. Somé recorded:

> I was so shocked. That was the first time I was brought face to face with what is done here to people exhibiting the same symptoms I've seen in my village." What struck Dr. Somé was that the attention given to such symptoms was based on pathology, on the idea that the condition is something that needs to stop. This was in complete opposition to the way his culture views such a situation. As he looked around the stark ward at the patients, some in straitjackets, some zoned out on medications, others screaming, he observed to himself, "So this is how the healers who are attempting to be born are treated in this culture. What a loss! What a loss that a person who is finally being aligned with a power from the other world is just being wasted" (Love, 2014, p. 2)

Dr. Somé explains how he saw "beings" and "entities" hanging around the patients and causing the crisis. He perceived that the entities were trying to get the medications and their effects out of their beings in order to proceed with the merging of the energy. In the Dagara tradition the whole community helps the person in dealing with these energies but Dr. Somé observes: "The Western culture has consistently ignored the birth of the healer. Consequently, there will be a tendency from the other world to keep trying as many people as possible in an attempt to get somebody's attention. They have to try harder" (Love, 2014, p. 3).

A large part of helping with such a crisis involves providing a context for understanding the experience. It will probably also involve providing social support, acceptance, and reassurance. It is also helpful to encourage the person in crisis to ground himself or herself by bathing, eating healthy foods, and spending time with nature. Shamanic traditions provide the person with access to different types of natural energies – rivers, mountains, trees and so forth. They also used rituals such as releasing symbols in bonfires and getting in touch with ancestors.

Such a contrast to Western approaches is striking; because in Western psychiatry a person in crisis is sedated with medications and told that their perceptions are wrong while depriving them from any real support for understanding the experience.

Another way to say this, which may make more sense to the Western mind, is that we in the West are not trained in how to deal or even taught to acknowledge the existence of psychic phenomena, the spiritual world. In fact, psychic abilities are denigrated. When energies from the spiritual world emerge in a Western psyche, that individual is completely unequipped to integrate them or

153

even recognize what is happening. The result can be terrifying. Without the proper context for and assistance in dealing with the breakthrough from another level of reality, for all practical purposes, the person is insane. Heavy dosing with anti-psychotic of drugs compounds the problem and prevents the integration that could lead to soul development and growth in the individual who has received these energies (Love, 2014, p. 2).

Episodes of unitive-consciousness (peak experiences)

A sense of unitive consciousness which is also called a mystical experience or a peak experience involves a sense of unity or awareness that everything is connected. It involves a transcendence of time and space and a sense of sacredness about all things along euphoria and a positive relationship with the divine. For many it includes a loss of ego functioning, alterations in one's perceptions of space and time and an experience of accessing the spiritual dimension.

The prominent psychologist Abraham Maslow (1964) described such experiences as "peak experiences" and placed them at the apex of his famous hierarchy of needs – even above self-actualization. Another psychologist, Walter Pahnke (1966), described the basic characteristics of a mystical or peak experience as a sense of unity both inner and out, strong positive emotions, transcendence of time and space, a sense of sacredness (numinosity), paradoxical awareness, objectivity and reality of insights, positive after effects, and ineffability.

Such experiences occur in non-ordinary states of consciousness but are mostly not intentionally induced but rather are unexpected and spontaneous. Neumann (1964)

154

defines the mystical experience as the "upheaval of the total personality". Mystical experiences are common enough to be seen regularly by psychotherapists. At least 4.5% of psychotherapy clients have brought mystical experiences to therapy (Allman, et al, 1992).

As with other spiritual experiences, it is useful to provide support and context. Some may be helped by dealing with every day issues – hygiene, housecleaning, and chores. It can also be helpful to receive some bodywork such as massage or reflexology, or to engage in rituals or to spend time writing down their thoughts or dreams.

Psychological Renewal through return to the center

Psychological renewal may involve the activation of a central archetype and an inner experience involving oneself in the center of the world. John Weir Perry (1974, 1976, 1998) has described the "renewal process" as a cosmic conflict that involves great clashes of opposites including polarities such as good and evil, light and darkness, good and evil, male and female, and even God and the Devil. The experience may involve images or experiences of death, the afterlife, or a return to creation. It can also involve identification with God.

This can easily be mistaken for psychosis by psychiatrists and others who follow the materialistic model of psychiatry regardless of their particular discipline. But, such an experience may have been the transformational point for many of those who are regarded as prophets and spiritual teachers. Certainly we can see elements of this renewal process in what we know of the lives of Moses, Zarathustra, Ezekiel, Elijah, and the apostle John. In more recent times we find elements of this process in the Mormon Prophet Joseph Smith. There is also the Sufi martyr, al-Hallaj, who declared – *ana'l Haqq* – "I am the Truth." And even possibly Jesus who declared "I am the Way, the Truth, and the Light."

Psychic opening

A psychic opening may involve the onset of psychic abilities or experiences such as telepathy, clairvoyance, precognition, psychokinesis, out-of-body-experiences (OOBEs), visions, and synchronicities. Psychic experiences are extremely common. In fact the majority of the population has had some sort of psychic experience like ESP and the percentage is increasing (Gallup, 1987).

The occurrences of paranormal experiences, although often downplayed or denied in certain settings are frequently reported informally. Many people report being visited by dead relatives or having premonitions. Near-death experiences including out-of-body experiences are more common than ever. Remote viewing has been studied and validated by scientists and even used by hard-headed no-nonsense law enforcement agencies and the intelligence community.

But in spite of the large number of reports and the huge number of experiments and studies devoted to psychic phenomena, society in general and "science" as an institution discounts the evidence. Such a context discourages the reporting, discussion, or honest investigation of such phenomenon. And the reporting becomes limited to small segments of society or to private discussions among trusted confidantes. If people experience a startling or profound experience then they may have difficulty making sense of it. They may come to doubt their own sanity. They may try to rationalize it away by denying their own experience. William James said: "The ignoring of data is, in fact, the easiest and most popular mode of obtaining unity in one's thought (James, 1978, p. 37). Unfortunately the cost of such unity of thought is high because it separates us from our experience and denies us access to greater progress.

People who have psychic experiences will need support and acknowledgment as do others experiencing spiritual emergence. They may need information as well to help them normalize the experience.

But is it real?

This question – is it real? – reflects the mindset of an antiquated, materialistic approach to science. The response is based on the inquirer's ability to make sense of the perception. In other words if "it" fits in with the perceiver's preconceived notions then it is real. If it does not then it is not real. In many cases the inquirer is compelled to find "a logical explanation" which is to say an explanation that confirms preconceptions and beliefs in fundamentalistic materialism. These are not productive ways of research since they start by excluding anything and everything that does not fit an already existing model. Yet many so-called scientists cling to these non-scientific approaches to examining new data and so exclude data that would contradict their existing models. That explains why it takes so long for scientific revolutions to take place. The heliocentric solar system, the existence of meteorites, the germ theory, evolution, quantum theory and other scientific revolutions took decades or more to be accepted by the scientific establishment and in some cases there are still dissenters to some of these. Their acceptance was not a matter of evidence or cogency of argument but rather simply of when they were trained and by whom. Max Planck, Nobel Laureate physicist and father of Quantum physics, said: "A new scientific truth does not triumph by convincing its opponents and making them see the light, but rather because its opponents eventually die, and a new generation grows up that is familiar with it" (Planck).

The evidence for psychic phenomena is overwhelming and undeniable. Reports of psychic phenomena are found in every culture and in every time period. To say dogmatically that there is no such thing as psychic phenomena puts us in the position of Galileo's inquisitors who refused to look through the telescope because they already knew what was there. To simply discount any and every psychic experience as false is unscientific. The fact that they are so widely reported means something is being experienced by millions of people over at least millennia. We may choose to disagree with the theologies and explanations that have been given by religions and folklore but we are still left with the undeniable facts: people old and young, throughout the history of humanity, and in every society and culture have reported experiencing psychic phenomena including telepathy, extrasensory perception, premonitions, remote viewing, communication with the dead or nonphysical entities, visions, and similar experiences under various names. And, quite frequently these experiences have been veridified or validated by witnesses or material evidence.

Some of the anecdotal evidence is startling in its accuracy and specificity. Pat Price was a retired officer who helped the Berkeley police in the Patty Hearst case. In research on remote viewing done at the Stanford Research Institute by Russell Targ and Hal Puthoff for the U.S. government Price was 90% accurate in his first attempt in remote viewing. His description of a swimming pool complex included its dimensions, size, location, and the function of the pools and the adjacent building (Powell, pp. 4-5).

William James, the father of American Psychology, was a scientist. He did not hesitate to explore the difficult or the occult. He attended séances and openly researched and wrote about mediums. His book *The Varieties of Religious Experience* is a masterpiece in the field of psychic research. James proposed that the brain could be a means of transmitting consciousness:

> Just as a prism alters incoming white light to form the characteristic colored spectrum, but is not the source of the light; and just as the lengths of the pipes of an organ determine how the inflowing air yields certain tones and not others, but are not, themselves, the source of the air, so too the brain may serve a permissive, transmissive, or expressive function, rather than solely a productive one, in terms of the thoughts, images, feelings, and other experiences it allows. (James, in Murphy and Ballou, 1960).

Aldous Huxley said much the same in 1954. He considered the brain to be a filter that primarily blocks consciousness rather than generates it and so allows us to register and express a narrow range of reality, which could be broadened during states of altered consciousness, such as meditation and dreams (Huxley, 1954).

And the research on psychic phenomena is not limited to philosophical conjecture and anecdotes. The Society for Psychical Research (SPR) was founded in 1882 and began gathering data on psychic phenomena. In an early report they found 149 cases of dream telepathy.

Over half of these were concerned with some sort of an emergency. Of reported spontaneous telepathic experiences about 65% have occurred in dreams (Rhine, 1981). Concerning dreams and telepathy, Carl Jung made the following comment:

> Another dream-determinant that deserves
> mention is telepathy. The authenticity of this
> phenomenon can no longer be disputed today. It
> is, of course, very simple to deny its existence
> without examining the evidence, but that is an
> unscientific procedure which is unworthy of
> notice. I have found by experience that telepathy
> does in fact influence dreams, as has been asserted
> since ancient times. Certain people are particularly
> sensitive in this respect.... The phenomenon
> undoubtedly exists, but the theory of it does not
> seem to me to be so simple (Jung, quoted in
> Powell, 25).

Upton Sinclair, the famous author, conducted research on telepathy that was rigorously scientific which he published in his book *Mental Radio*. Hans Berger invented the electroencephalogram (EEG) to investigate telepathy after his sister sent him a telegram saying she was concerned something bad had happened to him. Earlier that day he was almost killed when riding a horse (Powell, p. 7). Berthold Schwarz recorded coincidences that resembled telepathy within families including instances where children would blurt out comments as though in direct response to what the parent was silently thinking.

"Ganzfeld" is a German word which means "whole field" as in the whole field of consciousness. A Ganzfeld procedure is a mild form of sensory deprivation developed in 1964 by psychologists Mario Bertini, Helen Lewis, and

Herman Witkin to study altered states of consciousness. Charles Honorton, William Braud, and Adrian Parker applied the technique to study the psychic abilities of subjects in such a way that they could focus attention without competing with external stimulation. They affixed ping-pong ball halves over the eyes of one person (the receiver) while the person looked into a red light. They reduced auditory input by pink noise which is white noise with the high-frequency components filtered out. They were placed in a comfortable recliner and given hypnotic-like suggestions. Another person, the sender, looked at a picture and attempted to mentally transmit it to the receiver while the receiver was in the ganzfeld state (Powell, p. 34). The results confirmed psychic phenomena well beyond what would be expected by change.

In an experiment conducted by Adrian Parker and Joakim Westerlund at the University of Gothenburg in Sweden "receivers" were placed in isolation with minimal sensory input, to prevent interference. "Senders" were placed in an isolated room where they watched a film. The receivers meanwhile made comments on what information came to mind. A recording was made in real-time of the receivers' comments and later played along with the film for analysis. One participant described accurately, in real time, a full sequence of events as they occurred in the film (Parker, 2003).

From 1974 to 2004, 88 ganzfeld experiments were performed and 1008 of the 3145 trials were hits. The combined hit rate was 32% which is 7% higher than the 25% that would be expected by chance. The odds against such results being due to chance are about 29 quintillion to one. These and other experiments have been reported on by Dean Radin, an experimental parapsychologist, in his book *Entangled Minds: Extrasensory Experiences in a Quantum Reality.*

Matter versus Spirit

The so-called "scientific" view says there is nothing but matter. Everything is matter. There is no spirit, no mind, no consciousness. All of these non-material things are by definition – nothing. At least they are nothing more than epiphenomena of matter which is to say illusions. They are dogmatic about this – no soul, no mind, no spirit, no consciousness. So anything that implies the existence of these things is just wrong – by definition.

That position is of course not scientific at all. It is dogmatic and based solely on faith. It refuses to consider data and refuses to even consider anything that lies outside its narrow definition of "reality". This position is a recent deviation in the history of science. The greats of science for the most part acknowledged the role of consciousness and the spirit. Only recently has science been subverted by fundamentalist, materialistic atheism. Consider the words of the Nobel Laureate father of Quantum Theory:

> I regard consciousness as fundamental. I regard
> matter as derivative from consciousness. We
> cannot get behind consciousness. Everything that
> we talk about, everything that we regard as
> existing, postulates consciousness (Planck).

And while the dogmatic materialists rant about laws, real scientists like Max Planck steadily undermine the materialist view with new, almost mystical understandings like relativity, the uncertainty principle, non-local causality, and quantum leaps. Instead of referring to rigid physical laws the quantum physicists cast doubts over the entire structure of the cosmos: "We have no right to assume that any physical laws exist, or if they ever existed up to now, that they will continue to exist in a similar manner in the future" (Planck). And even more bluntly to doubt the very presence of matter: "As a man who has devoted his whole life to the most clear headed science, to the study of matter, I can tell you as a result of my research about atoms this much: There is no matter as such" (Planck).

Further quantum physics points to the underlying unity and connection of the Universe. The statements of physicists seem almost to echo the poetry of mystics in their descriptions of the Unity of all things.

> Quantum theory thus reveals a basic oneness of the universe.... As we penetrate into matter, nature does not show us any isolated 'basic building blocks,' but rather appears as a complicated web of relations between the various parts of the whole" (Capra, 2000, p. 68)

So we see that real science is far from dogmatic and can even go opposite from the "rationality" of the fundamentalistic materialists. William James was a true scientist and so was willing to explore all the data boldly and adventurously. He said:

> Matter might *everywhere* make mind conscious of what matter was doing, and mind might then everywhere either acquiesce in the performances, or encourage, hinder, or redirect them" (James, 1988, p. 428).

Past life experience

Karmic patterns or past life memories may involve recall of dramatic experiences of past lives including birth events. These may be intense emotional experiences of birth, torture, death, memories of family members or ancient cultures. These memories often illuminate present life difficulties, irrational fears, habits, and interpersonal dynamics. During a karmic crisis there are likely to be strong emotions along with physical sensations and even visions that intrude into daily life. There may be spontaneous recall of memories from past lives. There may be a tendency to act in certain ways toward others that are recognized from other roles in other lives. These emotions, memories, and actions can interfere with daily function or be acted on inappropriately.

As with psychic opening, the most difficult thing about a karmic crisis can be acceptance and intellectual integration. This is especially so for people with belief systems that are strongly opposed to a belief in reincarnation – like Fundamentalist Christians or "rational" people who feel that everything must be explained within the confines of materialistic science.

As with other crises, the helper must help slow the process down. There is no need to force an interpretation but it is perfectly acceptable to provide information. It is also important to help the client assess daily performance and continue to function well in daily life.

Communication with spirit guides and channeling

Similar to psychic opening, channeling and communicating with spirit guides involves in some way communication with unseen, non-hostile beings. It can take place during a trance state during which these beings can speak through the person in trance. They can also involve a more direct two-way communication in which the person "hears" the messages from the non-physical entity.

Channeling or mediumship has a long and distinguished history within psychology. Some of the most distinguished psychologists have studied and written about these subjects. A short list would include Wilhelm Wundt who established the first psychological laboratory in Europe, Thomas Flournoy who influenced Carl Jung among others, William James who is considered the father of American psychology and who studied mediums and séances, and Carl Jung who even wrote his doctoral dissertation on mediums.

In addition to studying various aspects of channeling, Jung also had a spirit guide. He was not alone. Beginning with the rise of Spiritualism many people including some of the great and famous have been attracted to these phenomena. And there have been a proliferation of channeled books including those by Jane Robert "Seth", and Pat Rodegast "Emmanuel". *A Course in Miracles* was and is widely read and studied as are the books channeled by "Abraham".

Like psychic opening and past life experiences the biggest problem with a person who communicates with spirit guides is the problem of acceptance and integration. The helper can provide information while helping the person in crisis accurately assess daily issues.

Jung was strongly influenced by Théodore Flournoy as were many others in the early twentieth century. Jung said of Flournoy: "During the time of my relationship to Freud I found a fatherly friend in Théodore Flournoy" (Jung in Forward to Flournoy, p. ix). And he noted: "In 1912 I induced Flournoy to attend the congress in Munich, at which the break between Freud and myself took place. His presence was an important support to me" (Ibid, p. ix). Flournoy himself was influenced by the pragmatism of William James (ibid, p. x).

James, Flournoy, and Jung were only three of many psychologists who were interested in channeling and mediums. Though these three participated in many séances and conducted serious research of this sort of phenomena there were many others who were interested in the subject.

At end (sic) of the nineteenth century, many of the leading psychologists – Freud, Jung, Ferenczi, Bleuler, James, Myers,, Janet, Bergson, Stanley Hall, Schrenck-Notzing, Moll, Dessoir, Richet, and Flournoy – frequented mediums. It is hard today to imagine that some of the most crucial questions of the 'new' psychology were played out in the séance, nor how such men could have been so fascinated by the spirits. What took place in the séances enthralled the leading minds of the time, and had a crucial bearing on many of the most significant aspects of twentieth-century psychology, linguistics, philosophy, psychoanalysis, literature, and painting, not to mention psychical research. For a while crucial issues in these disciplines found themselves played out in the transports of the mediumistic trance. A form of transvaluation took place" (Sonu Shamdasani, "Encountering Hélène: Thèodore Flournoy and the Genesis of Subliminal Psychology" Introduction to Flournoy. Pp. xi-xii).

Near Death Experience

Near death experiences (NDE) are becoming increasingly common because of improved medical technology. People who would have simply been dead a century ago may today be revived and a significant percentage of them report near death experiences (perhaps more accurately described as after clinical death experiences). These experiences often involve out-of-body-experiences (OOBE) during which the person can accurately report on things observed while they were clinically dead. They also involve a life review and a sense of peace for many. Most significantly they are followed by profound and persistent personality changes (Flynn, 1982). The NDE often includes events with paranormal features. In one study, 75% of the subjects reported out-of-body experiences, 49% reported an apparitional experience, and 21% reported being the subject of someone else's psychic experience during the NDE (Greyson and Stevenson, 1980). Other researchers have presented evidence for the objective reality of the experience (Grosso, 1981). Ring and his colleagues have provided numerous insights through research into NDEs. These include the occurrence of a number of psychic phenomena associated with NDEs including remote viewing, clairvoyance, and an increased occurrence of synchronicities (Ring, 1982, 1985; Ring and Valerino, 1998; Ring and Cooper, 1999). Apart from the inevitable pathological labels of psychiatry such as labeling synchronicities as delusions of reference and most other things as psychosis, another issue that arises with NDEs is the uncontrolled nature of post-NDE psychic experiences. Ring has proposed that the paranormal aspects of the NDE suggest the need for better models to account for psychospiritual functioning (Ring, 1981, 1982). In a review of the literature, Bruce Greyson, a past president of the International Association of Near-Death Studies and professor of psychiatry concluded:

> These data may be interpreted as evidence that NDEs somehow produce an increase in psychic experiences, presumably by facilitating communication with an individual's latent sensitivities or with some alternative reality.

Another interpretation compatible with these data is that the NDE may merely increase an individual's awareness of, or ability to recognize, those paranormal   abilities he or she always had (Greyson, 1983).

Close encounters with UFOs

"Reality is that which, when you stop believing in it, doesn't go away."
                                    -    Philip K. Dick (1928-1982)

Close encounters with UFOs may involve close contact during which the person sees and communicates with aliens. It can be pleasant or it can be frightening and unpleasant. It can even involve abduction by aliens during which there is intrusive physical examination and even sexual activity. These experiences are often accompanied by lost time, suppressed memories, and other signs.

In 1961 Betty and Barney Hill were driving near their home in New Hampshire when they saw a UFO. Subsequent to that they realized they were missing time from their recollection of the event and afterwards Barney experienced insomnia and nightmares. Two years later they saw a psychologist for a non-related issue that was not a psychiatric illness. Under hypnosis they reported being taken up by small gray beings with large eyes and of being examined and tested in a laboratory. Since then thousands of similar reports have occurred. The people involved usually do not seek therapy for alien abduction but they do experience nightmares, general anxiety, strange memories, panic attacks, and missing time.

Some of these reports even involve multiple people. Travis Walter in the late 1970s was missing in

Arizona for five days. A murder investigation was initiated before he was found miles away from where he was last seen. Several members of his logging crew reported seeing a UFO take him up in a beam of light. Such reports are widespread and plentiful. Dr. Jacque Vallee, the model for the expert in the movie *Close Encounters of the Third Kind,* documented many in his 1969 book *Passport to Magonia.*

To me these reports become even more interesting when compared to the much older stories of fairy abductions. Fairy abductions often involve conical hills or caverns which we might see as analogous to laboratories or spaceships. They also involve "fairy bruising" just as alleged alien abductions involve physical evidence of alien contact. And there are reports of gaps in the memory and even sex with the abductors.

The question that always arises when the subject of UFOs arises is whether or not they are real. (The question is not so common with fairy stories but then nowadays neither are the stories). By real the questioner usually means – are there intelligent beings from another planet visiting our planet and occasionally abducting people? More sophisticated inquirers might point out other possibilities such as extra-dimensional beings. The skeptics may allude to hallucinations caused by electromagnetic phenomena on the earth's surface. None of these questions or explanations are particularly relevant to us and our subject. A more relevant response to the question of whether or not they are real would be to ask – A real what?

C.G. Jung although a protégé of Sigmund Freud and a product of a less technological century lived long enough to be become interested in UFOs and reports of alien contact. Incidentally one of the early important influences on Jung was Théodore Flournoy who conducted extensive research on the medium Catherine Muller. He published his studies in the book *From India to the Planet Mars* in 1899. It was a landmark book that explored spiritism, glossolalia, and considered other parapsychological phenomena. It influenced Jung to conduct his own search on a medium (one of his cousins) which became the basis for his doctoral dissertation in 1902.

Jung even wrote a book about UFOs – *Flying Saucers: A Modern Myth of Things Seen in the Skies*. He even addressed the question of their physical reality:

> As a psychologist, I am not qualified to contribute anything useful to the question of the physical reality of UFOs. I can concern myself only with their undoubted psychic aspects, and in what follows shall deal almost exclusively with their psychic concomitants (Jung, 1959, p. 7).

> But if it is a case of psychological projection, there must be a psychic cause for it. One can hardly suppose that anything of such worldwide incidence as the UFO legend is purely fortuitous and of no importance whatever (Jung, 1959, p. 23)

Possession States

Possession is a controversial phenomenon involving the feeling of being controlled by a spirit or demon. It can involve strange facial characteristics and gestures, glossolalia, along with speech and behaviors that are contrary to the person's values and normal behavior. It is a widespread phenomenon that has even seen an increase in the Western world during the twentieth century but its history is long and deep.

The practice of psychology has been involved with demonology in several ways. In a sense the science of psychology grew in part out of demonology. The descriptions of the victims of demons in books such as *Malleus Malificarum* were predecessors to the first scientific studies in psychopathology and direct ancestors to the current *Diagnostics and Statistics Manual* of the American Psychiatric Association. The writings of medieval theologians and magicians at times foreshadow the writings of modern psychologists. There have been fictional experts on demons as well, Van Helsing, in Bram Stoker's famous book and Van Helsing's "friend Arminius of Buda-Pesht" who was in real life Arminius Vambery, an Hungarian adventurer and folk-lore expert and friend of Stoker. But whether theologian or mage, factual or fictional, paranormal investigators, or demonologists of all kinds have to some extent begin students of human psychology.

And psychology has always had some concern with possession. As early as the late nineteenth century, Pierre Janet advocated exorcism or mock religious ceremonies to relieve some symptoms of mental illness. He also successfully cured a possessed man by speaking with the demon and tricking the demon into leaving (Rug, p. 196). Janet's younger contemporary, Sigmund Freud, even wrote a paper on a seventeenth century possession.

Some such as Aleister Crowley, the psychologically oriented mage, and Carl Jung, the magically oriented psychologist, have identified spirits and demons as identical with the processes of the mind. William James took a similar view: "If there are devils — if there are supernormal powers it is through the cracked self that they enter" (James, 1988, p. 72). Commenting on the teachings of Jung, Paul Levy observed: "...the psychic conditions which breed demons are as actively at work as ever. The demons have not really disappeared but have merely taken on another form: they have become unconscious psychic forces" (Levy, 2009).

Such a belief in no way negates the reality of demons or their actions. Others, less spirituality minded, might reduce demons and other spiritual phenomena to nothing more than mental processes. But even such extreme reductionistic positions still must admit the occurrence of experiences such as possession and haunting as subjective realities even if they do not admit them personally (Rug, p. 196).

Finally, it must be realized that those who work in the field of psychology – counselors, psychologists, and social workers – are among those most likely to be exposed to the victims of demons. Few, other than psychic investigators, magical practitioners, and clergy are as likely to deal directly with those issues. Of course, most counselors may not recognize demonic possession when they see it but that does not mean they will not be involved with it in some way.

Possession is frequently a "culture-bound syndrome" that involves the beliefs and practices of a given society or culture. It is important for the helper to be aware of cultural factors that deal with this particular crisis whether it be a particular Christian or other belief or a folk belief from another culture. In many cases the best way to help will be to access the resources within the person's culture that are there to support or help with such a crisis. At the very least, knowing something about the person's culture and beliefs will enable the helper to provide relevant support.

Of course not all possession is negative. In some cultures this is the method for communicating with benign spirits and is really more a matter of channeling than of possession as it is usually thought of. In either case the person can benefit from the usual process that involves accepting, supporting, and providing a safe environment.

Voodoo, curses, evil eye

Of course psychology has recognized for some time the reality of certain magical processes such as voodoo curses. At least modern science has conceded that a person might die from "voodoo death" because that person believes in the efficacy of the voodoo curse (Cannon, 1941). Psychology has relegated this to "the power of suggestion" and has conveniently ignored cases where the cursed person was not even aware of the curse.

Science has even recognized the reality of the voodoo practice of creating zombies. But, despite the scientific explanations of suggestion and drugs this must be considered magic – and terrifying magic at that (Davis, 1985).

> Australian Aborigines had a tradition of pointing a bone at someone to cast a spell. The man who discovers that he is being boned is, indeed, a pitiable sight. He stands aghast, with his eyes staring at the treacherous pointer, and with his hands lifted as though to ward off the lethal medium, which he imagines is pouring into his body. His cheeks blanch and his eyes become glassy, and the expression of his face becomes horribly distorted.... He attempts to shriek but usually the sound chokes in his throat, and all that one might see is a froth at his mouth. His body begins to tremble and the muscles twist

involuntarily. He sways backwards and falls to the ground, and after a short time appears to be in a swoon; but soon after he writhes as if in mortal agony, and covering his face with his hands, begins to moan.... His death is only a matter of comparatively short time (Basedow, 1925).

Walter B. Cannon (1942) found that there was power in the *tapu* of the Maoris in New Zealand. He described it as "a fatal power of the imagination working through unmitigated terror". He documented how curses result in various physiological effects including reduced blood volume, decreased appetite, and ultimately death. His initial paper has stood the test of time and has gained a better understanding over time with an increased understanding of the brain (Sterbberg, 2002). Dr. Erich Menninger von Leachenthal of Vienna reported several instances of sudden death through fright (Menninger, 1948).

The description of the general adaptation syndrome which is now known as the stress response by Hans Selye did not occur until after the publication of Cannon's famous paper. Since then there has been added a vast body of knowledge to Selye's initial description which shows the importance of the hypothalamus in the stress response along with the secretion of various hormones and their effect on the body. This understanding of the physiological response systems linking the body with the emotions is also the foundation of our developing understanding of the connection of the mind and body. This includes such things as the placebo effect and the "fight or flight response", a term invented by Cannon.

In modern Western society the same phenomena is familiar. Just as much of the healing that occurs in modern medicine is due to placebo effect, much of the illness occurs from the negative aspect of the same mechanism. We call the negative aspect "nocebo" and any honest appraisal has to recognize the strong role this plays in the inappropriately named healthcare system.

> Seventy-four percent of the complaints patients bring to medical clinics are of unknown origin and are probably caused by 'psychosocial' factors, according to a study reported by Dr. Kurt Kroenke of the Uniformed Services University of Health Sciences in Bethesda, Maryland, and A. David Mangelsdorff, PhD., MPH, of the Brooke Army Medical Center in Houston, Texas. (Benson, 1996, p. 49;   Kroenke and Mangelsdorff, 1989).

It is also widely recognized that the nocebo effect is closely related to the emotional and physiological effects of stress. As Herbert Benson said: "Other studies indicate that between 60 and 90 percent of all our population's visits to doctor's offices are stress-related and probably cannot be detected much less treated effectively with the medications and procedures on which the medical profession relies almost exclusively" (Benson, 1996, pp. 49-50).

To help with such situations as well as with possession, the helper must become informed of the person's beliefs and culture. Most cultures that allow for such phenomena will also have remedies and protections. It is useful and appropriate to remind or assist the person in crisis with such remedies but it is not always appropriate to assume the role of priest or shaman. It is often much more appropriate to consult with a priest,

175

minister, healer, shaman, or other traditional helper within that cultural worldview. In any case the person should be supported and encouraged as in any such crisis. This would include helping them understand and integrate the experience as a form of growth or learning.

Spiritual and Religious Issues that are not necessarily emergencies (but might be)

There are a number of issues that are impacted on by spiritual and religious practices. These include such things as dealing with death and grief, aging, birth, divorce, other developmental changes, questions regarding one's faith, and other issues dealing directly with faith, belief, and the religious community. These do not necessarily lead to spiritual or emotional crisis but they can. Other issues relating to religion can have profound effects and might lead to crisis. These could include spiritual abuse, cult membership, moral panic, and issues involving acceptance of gays, treatment of women, and one's role in the faith community or larger society.

Spiritual Abuse

Though not necessarily a trigger for spiritual emergence, spiritual abuse can certainly trigger a crisis and a spiritual emergency. Spiritual abuse describes the situation where a person in spiritual authority misuses their authority to coerce or manipulate others. The sexual abuse committed by certain Catholic priests certainly falls in this category but there are many more examples. Extreme examples would include Jim Jones, Charles Manson, and Marshall Applegate. The LDS Church's vendetta against certain academics and intellectuals would be another example. Then there are gurus and shamans who have used their authority to gain money and sexual favors. The problem is universal and found not just in religions and spiritual situations but also within business, education, and the military. A good introduction to this issue is *The Subtle Power of Spiritual Abuse* by Jeff Van Vondern.

Spiritually abusive organizations tend to over-emphasis authority in the form of a religious hierarchy or leader and so are hierarchal with authority based on position rather than on moral authority. Followers might even be told that their obedience to leaders will be rewarded even if the leaders are wrong. They are not allowed to judge or criticize leaders.

Such authority-oriented hierarchal organizations are invested in avoiding criticism – especially in public. They often misrepresent history to create the image they choose. They deny mistakes or character flaws in their leaders even to the point of cover up in order to validate their authority. They tend to emphasize high legalistic standards of thought and behavior for members as a means of emphasizing the inferiority of members to leaders.

The suppression of criticism follows from the need to maintain authority. Any questions, dissent or even discussion can be framed as apostasy with the person who raises the issue seen as the problem rather than the issue that was raised. Issues are settled from top down. Even identifying blatant errors can be seen as a lack of faith and a challenge to authority.

The problem often includes unspoken rules and a lack of balanced power. At times it is the result of people pretending to a level of spiritual advancement to which they have not achieved. It may at other times simply be a matter of human nature and temptation. In either case there are at least two people in crisis and sometimes whole congregations and communities.

The helper's task is to help them to understand, integrate, and heal. To help with this it is important to understand and respect the culture and beliefs of the system or systems involved. To do this adequately will often require the helper to consult with spiritual teachers or religious providers within that culture. As obvious as this might seem, mental health providers seldom consult with spiritual teachers even when dealing with religious and spiritual issues (Larson, et al, 1988). Many ministers have training that will help with any intervention and may have training beyond that of the helper. In some circles this is known as pastoral crisis intervention, which is defined as "...the functional integration of any and all religious, spiritual and pastoral resources with the assessment and intervention technologies germane to the practice of emergency mental health" (Everly, 2000, p. 2) or "the functional integration of psychological crisis intervention with pastoral care (ibid, p. 1). I prefer the latter definition since it seems less likely to lead to medication and leans more toward spiritual intervention – acceptance, support, encouragement and other spiritual tools.

Religious Trauma Syndrome (RTS)

Religious Trauma Syndrome is a term coined by Dr. Marlene Winell in 2011 that grew from her personal experience as the daughter of Pentacostal missionaries as well as from her professional work as a psychologist. Over the past twenty years she has counseled people who have had been damaged by experiences in various fundamentalist and evangelical churches. Winell describes the harmful experiences with religion as "...the result of two things: immersion in a controlling religion and the secondary impact of leaving a religious group (Tarico, 2013, p. 2). The harmful results are not just sexual or physical abuse but can include fear, anxiety, panic attacks, and a perception of one's spiritual deficiency.

Part of the problem with the RTS label and Winell's approach is that it pathologizes entire groups of people and their belief systems. To a certain extent it takes the black-and-white approach that Winell describes as a problem within these religions. WInell's response to such criticism is: "Saying that someone is trying to pathologize authoritarian religion is like saying someone pathologized eating disorders by naming them" (Tarico, 2013, p. 5). But unfortunately the RTS label is much more than a critique of the abuse of authority as in spiritual abuse. It is a wholesale criticism of certain religions and their beliefs.

There does not seem to be any effort to look for the positive and constructive aspects of these religions. Rather the focus is on attacking the theology and culture of these groups as the source of only destructive and painful influences. Such an approach leads to support groups where participants who are "recovering from religion" air their grievances and criticize their former faith group. Little room is left for a constructive use of spirituality or reconciliation with their original faith or culture.

Such a negative approach does not lead to healing and is too simplistic to address in any meaningful way the issues of individuals. It is easy to target Pentacostals, Evangelicals, Mormons, Catholics or other groups and to blame any or all issues on their deficiencies. But such an approach fails to recognize the positive role played by religion in the lives of most of the members of these groups. Within each of the targeted groups there are many who have experienced great spiritual growth and happiness because of the teachings of their religion.

The RTS label tends to encourage non-believers or former believers to critique and argue with the doctrines of their faith. While it is certainly legitimate to encourage people to think rigorously and to think seriously about their beliefs, it is not the role of the helper to simply discount the beliefs of legitimate religions.

Specific doctrines criticized by those who advocate the RTS label include beliefs in hell and repentance. They refer to those who literally advocate the principle of "spare the rod and spoil the child" or "if thy eye offend thee, pluck it out." I agree that a literal interpretation should be avoided and from my interactions with people of many faiths I know that the mature informed believers of all faiths approach these teachings much more compassionately and flexibly than do the critics of religion.

Advocates for the RTS label accuse Born-again Christianity and Catholicism of teaching people they are weak and dependent because of their use of phrases such as "lean not unto your own understanding" or "trust and obey". In other words they consider such principles as humility, seeking Divine wisdom, loyalty, and devotion as roads to learned helplessness. The RTS approach aligns itself with the anti-religious and the atheists. It makes personal struggles a political issue rather than a matter of introspection, meditation, prayer, service, and compassion.

On the other hand, it is true that people can be and sometimes are damaged by religious teachings. As we saw above, spiritual abuse is a problem. When people have a simplistic understanding of certain doctrines, of course, they are liable to apply that understanding in an inadequate or even damaging manner. But, to say that there are levels of understanding does not lead immediately to the demonization and pathologizing of whole churches and religions. It leads instead to the need for greater understanding and better more informed efforts by those who teach and lead. It is the difference between – "I'm screwed up because of my church" – to "what must I do to change?" Simply deferring responsibility onto any external influence whether church, state, family, or event denies the individual's own capacity to change, heal, learn, grow, think, and ultimately determine his or her own course in life.

A much better course when dealing with someone who feels damaged by the teachings of a given church or faith is to explore with them their understanding of the meaning of certain teachings. If you are not an expert in their beliefs then guide them in gaining better information. Access an expert or refer to an appropriate representative of the faith. Most importantly help them to explore rigorously the meaning of their belief.

Rather than simply condemning and arguing engage in the process of spiritual exploration. Look for and find the constructive teachings. If in the end they should decide to leave their faith, let it be a peaceful and gentle leaving. Rancor, bad-feelings, blaming, becoming an "anti-" something, or a "recovering" something leaves one in a negative place. It leaves one connected to a perception of being damaged, vulnerable, and out of control. The helper's job is to help the person experience growth along with an increase of positive emotions and understanding.

Moral Panic

　　　Related loosely to the concepts of Possession, Religious Trauma Syndrome, and Spiritual Abuse is the concept of moral panic. Moral panic has been "defined as an episode, often triggered by alarming media stories and reinforced by reactive laws and public policy, of exaggerated or misdirected public concern, anxiety, fear, or anger over a perceived threat to social order" (Krinsky, n.d.). Moral panics are characterized by volatility, hostility, consensus, disproportionality and measurable concern. More simply it can be thought of as a type of public madness, a delusion of crowds.

　　　Jeffrey Victor has provided another useful summary of the nature of moral panics:

> In brief, a moral panic is a form of collective behavior characterized by suddenly increased concern and hostility in a significant segment of a society, in reaction to widespread beliefs about a newly perceived threat from moral deviants. Careful, empirical examination at a later time, however, reveals that the perceived threat was greatly exaggerated or non-existent. A moral panic often gives rise to social movements aimed at eliminating the threatening deviants and may generate moral crusades and political struggles over use of the law to suppress the dangerous deviants. Local rumor-panics, riots and ethnic programs may occur in reaction to belief in the threat. However, such dramatic behavior is not an essential element of the collective behavior. Belief, not emotion, is the motivational dimension of a moral panic. The essence of the moral panic

is that significant segments of a society are reacting to a socially constructed threat from moral deviants. The main observable behavior during a moral panic is the communication of claims, accusations and rumors (Victor, 1998, p. 2).

There are many examples of moral panic throughout history. The blood libel against the Jews by Apion in the early first century of the Common Era was a moral panic as were the persecutions against the Christians during the Roman Empire. The European witch-hunt was a moral panic that resulted in over a hundred thousand deaths. Though much smaller the seventeenth century Massachusetts witch-hunt was also a moral panic. More recently there was the Red Scare that resulted in McCarthyism in twentieth century America that caused thousands to be labeled subversive and to lose their jobs. The War on Drugs is another which like the others is largely baseless and caused disproportionate harm to many people.

A classic moral panic began in the 1980s and lasted into the early 1990s. This was the day-care sex abuse hysteria that alleged a widespread conspiracy of Satanic cults working secretively in day-care centers to ritually abuse children and to kill thousands of people. The panic was based largely on the testimony of children that was elicited largely as repressed memories by investigators. Although many suffered personally and professionally from these allegations, no evidence of widespread abuse, Satanic Cults, or the massacre of thousands was ever discovered.

Although not all moral panics are as widespread as the day-care sex abuse hysteria they all tend to create misery and suffering wherever they occur. False or groundless beliefs influence public policy and the behavior of people toward groups that in reality pose no threat. The False Memory Syndrome which was recognized in large part because of the false memories of children in the alleged Satanic abuse still plays a factor in our society. Many lives have been impacted by false memories "recovered" by case workers and therapists. Perhaps even worse is that many people have been deprived of healing and personal growth by a belief that recovery of repressed memories is essential for overcoming problems and personal growth. The culprits are often incompetent therapists and self-help books as well as pop psychology as perpetuated by media and folklore.

The role of the helper is to restore reason and balance by providing some reality testing. Help the person to question and examine rumors. Examine sources of rumors and do reality testing by finding believable sources. Help them to slow down and think through decisions that could result in harm to others or to their own emotional and spiritual well-being. More especially it is the role of the professional helper to be professional and this includes being competent. A therapist or other professional helper who succeeds only in increasing misery and in maintaining a client in perpetual therapy should either improve his or her skills or pursue a different career. Competent therapy must include a set of beliefs that encourages healing and emotional growth. These beliefs at a minimum should include a belief in the possibility of improvement and personal resilience. Any beliefs that do not encourage such hope are detrimental like the popular self-help book described by one commentator that "....encourages the simpleminded scientifically illiterate misconception that the explanation for symptoms of unhappiness, depression, and almost any other complaint *must* be the presence of repressed memories, and invites women to rewrite their entire life and family histories..." (The Courage). Such beliefs and approaches must be avoided by anyone who is interested in truly helping others.

Conversion or Loss of Faith

Conversion occurs when someone changes from one religion (or no religion) to another. Like most things conversion can refer to a range of actions. It can range from a mystical or "religious experience" to a matter of choosing a church that is close to one's house. It might involve classes and lengthy training as with preparation for conversion to Judaism or it could be fairly quick and easy as with reciting the Shahada in Islam or being welcomed to the church in many Protestant churches. It can involve active proselytizing and persuasion as with the Mormons or more low-key and subtle invitations. It could result from personal study and prayer or it could be part of a mass movement like the revivals of the Great Awakening or the Billy Graham Crusades.

In most cases there is a strong social or cultural component. People hold the religious beliefs they were raised in and when they do convert to another faith it tends to be one that is similar (at least to an outsider). Protestants switch to other Protestant faiths or at least to other Christian faiths. Faith groups tend to be culturally homogeneous (not surprising since religion too is an aspect of cultural). Even with religions that have greater diversity the actual practice of religion tends to be homogeneous. Individual Catholic Churches tend to be either Hispanic or White for example. Of course this is influenced by the ethnic and cultural makeup of the community which is a major influence on religious choice.

All of these factors – personal, spiritual, cultural, familial, and in some cases economic and political – make the change of religion a serious action. It has impacts on virtually every area of life. In some cases it can result in broken relationships, family splits, and even loss of job and ostracism by the community and others.

For these reasons, along with spiritual experiences, conversion can result in a personal crisis that requires considerable support from the new faith community and possibly from other helpers as well. Some faith communities encourage a split and even non-contact with family and friends who are non-believers. This can exacerbate the sense of loss and loneliness for the new convert. This isolation may increase other aspects of the person's crisis.

A person who breaks with a faith group whether due to spiritual abuse, a cult experience, or from normal spiritual exploration and growth may experience a number of issues. These include isolation and loneliness from changing the social environment. There can also be depression due to self-doubt and arising from teachings about apostasy. The person may experience a period in which it is difficult to make decisions or plans. They may experience "floating" in which there are lapses back into the previous group mindset that are triggered by settings, words, music, or symbols. Some may find it difficult to talk about their involvement with the previous group due to shame, fear, guilt, or bitterness. There are also often interpersonal issues communicating, making new friends, fitting in with a new group that may be due in part to lack of trust and suspicion or simply part of the process of adjusting to a new group.

The helper may need to help the person examine "teachings" that encourage withdrawal and isolation. For example, if they believe they must withdraw from others the helper might help them to examine how that would fit in with an admonition to evangelize or spread the word. Emotional support and connection may also be important for the convert and may require helping the convert to acculturate to the new religion and to access support and social activities within the new faith community.

The Dark Night of the Soul and Depression

Related to conversion is the concept of the Dark Night of the Soul since conversion is often preceded by a lengthy process of introspection. This may involve ruminations about one's lack of worthiness due to sin. It could include struggling with doubts. This is common to some degree for many adolescents although not to the extent that the term is normally used. It might not involve switching to another faith community but instead could be part of the acceptance and integration of the religion's values in one's own life. It could be part of a process of development and initiation.

The term "Dark Night of the Soul" (*La noche oscura del alma*) was originated by St. John of the Cross to describe the dark trial experienced by many mystics as part of their spiritual development. It is a spiritual term that is now part of the Roman Catholic tradition but clearly has applications in other paths as well. This dark night typically includes doubt and despair. It is a spiritual crisis that plays a part in a person's spiritual growth as an attempt is made to seek union with God. In addition to St. John of the Cross's poem and essay others have also left descriptions of the dark night. These include St. Thérèse of Liseaux, St. Paul of the Cross, and Mother Teresa.

Although often short in duration it can last for a long time. In the case of St. Paul of the Cross it lasted forty-five years.

The Dark Night of the Soul is a profound process on the spiritual path. It has elements which are similar to depression and so both might be considered together as aspects of spiritual emergence or emergency. As the psychiatrist Gerald May has commented: "But my experience is that people often experience depression and the dark night of the soul at the same time. To say the least, the dark night can be depressing" (May, 2005, p. 156). Dr. May is not the only person to consider depression in a spiritual light. Stefanie Sorrell in her book *Depression As A Spiritual Journey* makes the argument for depression being part of spiritual emergence and an important aspect of spiritual development (Sorrell, 2009).

In considering the dark night of the soul and depression we must consider all types of dark emotions such as grief, fear, doubt, guilt, shame, despair, or others. These and other dark emotions are not problems or symptoms but rather are part of the process of being human. Like the mystic's dark night they are part of the path to greater wisdom, empathy, compassion, and understanding. Unfortunately they are too likely to be perceived by today's society as a problem to be solved or worse yet a disease to be medicated.

Even when depression results from other causes such as trauma, loss, job loss, or drug use, it can be involved in spiritual emergence. Alister Hardy conducted research into the most common triggers for religious, spiritual, or mystical experiences. His research found that the most common trigger was depression or despair with the second being prayer or meditation, and the third being natural beauty (Hardy, 1979, p. 28).

Childbirth is sometimes followed by post-partum depression but it is frequently followed by feelings of tender emotions and even spiritual emergence. As a crisis counselor in Sacramento I met a man in the walk-in clinic who had recently experienced the addition of his first child to his life and family. He was a traditionally masculine man – reticent, stoic, tough – who when not working at his macho job enjoyed camping and hunting high in the mountain wilderness. He was convinced that he was having a "nervous breakdown" because he was feeling tender and even at times tearful. The intervention for him involved bringing him to an understanding of the importance of tenderness for future growth and for getting close to his child as she grew. In his case this was accomplished with a guided visualization.

To help someone who is dealing with dark emotions the focus is not on eliminating or curtailing these emotions but rather on experiencing them. It is through the experience of dark emotions that we gain wisdom, strength, empathy, patience, and enhanced spirituality.

Research into the role of religious affiliation with depression has found that people of Jewish descent, Pentacostals, and those with no affiliation have the highest rates of depression. It has also been found in the great majority of research studies that there is less depression and faster recovery with greater reduction of symptoms when there is a religious or spiritual intervention. Similarly the rate of suicide and attempted suicide is significantly lower with less depression, less anger, lower rates of substance abuse, greater social support, and better coping skills when there is religious or spiritual involvement (Plante, 2009).

This information is important to those who wish to help those who experience depression. Many of these professional helpers are already working in a religious context as pastoral counselors, chaplains, or clergy. It is estimated that community clergy spend about 15% of their time counseling. There are over 300,000 clergy in the United States not including another 100,000 full-time nuns and chaplains. This means that more than 140 million hours of therapy is provided by clergy per year. That is roughly equivalent to the entire membership of the American Psychological Association providing thirty-three hours a week of counseling a year. Although clergy provide the front-line services for mental health many of them receive no training. Providing them with tools for religious and spiritual based therapies would greatly improve the situation (Bonelli, Dew, et al., 2012).

In clinical trials performed to demonstrate the benefit of religious or spiritually integrated therapies for depression it was found that such approaches are more effective than non-spiritual approaches. In at least two trials it was found that therapy supplemented with teachings from the Quran and Islamic prayer were effective in treating depression among Muslims. A number of other psychospiritual interventions have been shown to bring significant benefits in the treatment of depression. These include meditation, religious forgiveness therapy, mantra chanting, spiritual coping therapy, spiritual-focused therapy, spiritual history taking, a spiritual program, 12-step spirituality program, spiritual direction, and others. It has also been found that religious and spiritual therapies do not need to be done by religious or spiritual therapists (Bonelli, Dew, et al, 2012).

Developmental Crisis

Perhaps related to the dark night of the soul is the concept of a developmental crisis since the dark night itself is part of the process of spiritual development. But other aspects of development can also impact us spiritually. As mentioned above childbirth can be followed by spiritual crisis or depression. Similarly other major points in development can act as initiations into a new phase of life and bring with it the same challenges that might attend a shamanic initiation. These can include starting school, graduating school, rites of passage in the church or community, starting a job, changing jobs, marriage, divorce, the empty nest, and the so-called mid-life crisis. In the mid-life crisis a person can experience anxiety or fear about aging and begin to question their activities, values, and choices in life. Intrinsically, it is a spiritual crisis that can cause a person to make significant changes in an attempt to regain youth, fend off aging or death, and to regain a sense of purpose or meaning in life.

Carl Jung commented on the spiritual aspect of this developmental crisis which he saw as universal in the latter half of life. Among his many comments concerning the need for the sense that life is worth living, that it has a purpose, is the following:

> Among all my patients in the second half of life —
> that is to say, over thirty-five—there has not been
> one whose problem in the last resort was not that
> of finding a religious outlook on life. It is safe to
> say that every one of them fell ill because he had
> lost what the living religions of every age have
> given their followers, and none of them has been
> really healed who did not regain his religious
> outlook. This of course has nothing whatever to do

with a particular creed or membership of a church (Jung, 1970, p. 509).

Psychedelics, Entheogens and Other Drugs

While spiritual emergencies may occur by the use of entheogens, they are not necessarily triggered by their use. Nor is the use of entheogens the only possible trigger for a spiritual crisis, as we have seen above. St. John of the Cross in particular addresses spiritual crisis from devotion and prayer resulting in the "dark night of the soul." The biographies of many mystics and religious leaders describe spiritual crises which may derive from meditation, devotional exercises, prayer and even from sudden insights brought on by observation and reading. This is apparent with John Bunyan, St. John of the Cross, and many other great mystics and religious leaders.

But certain drugs and plants can and do have profound effects on many people. These effects can be life-changing and a growing body of literature is available on the powerful spiritual and healing effect of certain entheogens. Nevertheless when taken in an inappropriate context or in an inappropriate dosage these substances can also have adverse effects. And, some drugs that affect the human mind are addictive or abused recreationally. Chief among these is alcohol.

Substance Abuse

Substance abuse is simply that of abusing a substance. That usually means the excessive use of a substance resulting in intoxication and or injury to the person who uses it. Addiction refers to the chronic abuse of a substance and according to the medical model this is a disease caused by dysfunction in one of various functions of the brain. There are other models. According to Carl Jung and the early Alcoholics Anonymous the problem of alcohol addiction has more to do with spiritual issues – or at least it was best treated as a spiritual issue. Another model of treatment is that of Harm Reduction therapy which teaches: "The essence of this model is the pragmatic recognition that treatment must meet active substance users 'where they are in terms of their needs and personal goals.' Thus harm reduction approaches embrace the full range of harm reducing goals including, but not limited to abstinence" (Tatarsky, 2003).

One of the most widely used addictive drugs in the world is alcohol. It is dangerous, destructive and costly for individuals, families, and society. Yet, as with anything when viewed from different perspectives it takes on different attributes. William James, the father of American Psychology and one of the first psychologists to seriously consider altered states of consciousness and spirituality as legitimate areas of study, alluded to spiritual and mystical aspects of alcohol use: "The sway of alcohol over mankind is unquestionable due to its power to stimulate the mystical faculties of human nature, usually crushed to earth by the cold facts and criticisms of the sober hour. Sobriety diminishes, discriminates, and says no; drunkenness expands, unites and says yes." There is evidence that the craving for drugs or alcohol is underlined by a craving for transcendence (Grof, 1987). Viktor Frankl, the author of *Man's Search for Meaning*, said: "Many people with addictions or depression lack meaning in life" (Frankl, 1959, p. 105).

Of course, William James was not the first to consider alcohol in a positive spiritual sense. The Bible has many references to alcohol in which it is considered a blessing and at least metaphorically considered a spiritual blessing. The mystical poetry of the Sufis is noted for its many references to wine as a symbol of mystical insight. Drunkenness in several traditions is used as an image of being close to the Divine.

According to Meher Baba many of India's insane, called the *Masts* or Drunkards, are in various states of spiritual evolution. Though used as a metaphor for spiritual advancement, intoxication is used by Meher Baba and others as a model or example of spiritual emergence. They become insane from meditative practices and from the sudden contact with a highly advanced spiritual being He refers to them as the God-Intoxicated:

> They are in a state of mental and physical disorder
> because their minds are overcome by strong
> spiritual energies that are far too much for them,
> forcing them to renounce the world, normal
> human habits and customs, and civilized society,
> and to live in a condition of chaos. They are
> psychological cases beyond the reach of
> psychoanalysis, because their condition is too
> advanced and obscure for any known procedures.
> Their minds are in some way shattered and their
> brains cannot fully function. Only a spiritual
> Master, says Baba, who is aware of the divine spirit
> that possesses them, which causes them to be unfit
> for normal society, can be of any help to them, and
> even his help reaches them with difficulty as they
> are virtually shut off from human contact. They are
> in the world but not of it. In Baba's terms they are
> 'God-intoxicated souls. (Purdom, 1964, p. 137)

According to William James the best treatment for dipsomania, an archaic term for alcoholism, is religiomania. He was not alone in that opinion. Carl Jung had a patient by the name of Roland H. who after exhausting other means sought out Jung for the treatment of alcoholism. He experienced some temporary improvement with Jung after a year in therapy but then relapsed. Jung said the case was hopeless and suggested to Roland that his only chance was to join a religious community and hope for a profound religious experience. Jung liked to say *Spiritus contra spiritum* in regards to the cure for alcoholism – that is, the Spirit against the spirits. Roland joined the Oxford Group, an evangelical movement which emphasized self-survey, confession, and service. He experienced a religious conversion and returned to New York where he continued his activity in the Oxford Group. He helped Edwin T. who in turn influenced his friend Bill Wilson. Bill had a powerful religious experience which included a vision of a worldwide chain-style fellowship of alcoholics helping each other.

Bill Wilson (or Bill W. as he is usually known) became the founder of Alcoholics Anonymous and carried on a correspondence with Carl Jung beginning in 1961. Shortly before the second international AA convention Bill W., after twenty years of sobriety, was introduced to LSD. In 1956 he first took LSD and continued its use with friends and acquaintances including clergymen and psychiatrists. Bill W. advocated the use of LSD to cure alcoholism because of it powerful potential for eliciting change (Wilson and Jung, 1963).

The AA board was shocked by his suggestion that LSD sessions should be introduced into the AA program. They rejected his proposal and he was eventually forced to leave the organization he helped to found.

Hallucinogen Intoxication

Hallucinogens are a class of drugs which are used to produce hallucinations. Commonly used hallucinogens include LSD, phencyclidines such as Ketamine and PCP, mescaline, MDMA (aka ecstasy), psilocybin and dimethyltryptamine (DMT). Several of these are the active agents derived from plants: LSD from the rye ergot, mescaline from cactuses, psilocybin from mushrooms, and DMT from ayahuasca and other plants. Many of the plants that can be used as hallucinogens are called entheogens, and are used in traditional rituals to bring on spiritual experiences. These include such plants or plant mixtures as ayahuasca (a mixture of the ayahuasca vine and the Chakruna leaf), datura (aka jimsonweed, toé, and other names), peyote, and San Pedro (also known as wachuma). These only represent a small number of the hallucinogens currently known.

Many issues with intoxication can be avoided by remembering the importance of set and setting when using hallucinogens. "Set" refers to the person's mind-set, emotions, and intentions when using such substances. Dark, foreboding, anxious feelings and thoughts are to be avoided. Conscious intentions that invoke pleasant experiences are encouraged.

Hallucinogen intoxication has many of the characteristics one might expect from other types of intoxication. Following recent ingestion there may occur disturbances of perception while still awake and attentive. These can include intensification of perception, depersonalization, derealization, illusions, synesthesias, and of course hallucinations. There may be marked anxiety or depression, ideas of reference, fear of losing one's mind, paranoia, or impaired judgment.

There will also be changes in thinking, judgment, and psychomotor behavior. There may also be physiological changes such as dilated pupils, increased heart rate, sweating, palpitations, blurring of vision, tremors, and incoordination. Some but not necessarily all of these may be present.

Physical addiction is not an issue and there is no evidence of any long-term damage. When helping someone who is intoxicated with hallucinogens the first step should be to assess for any immediate risk of physical danger to them or others. Take whatever steps are necessary to keep everyone safe. Stay with them and keep them safe and comfortable.

The important point to keep in mind when helping someone with such an experience is to be calm. Your calmness will help them to be calm. Hold their hands, if it's alright with them, and reassure them. Help them change the mood to one that is peaceful and calm. Help them to relax and enjoy while breathing deeply and slowly. Sometimes a change of scenery is useful. At the Burning Man festival they have a "chill tent" where those who need it can sit with helpers during acute intoxication. If possible provide animals for them to pet or play with. Another technique is to sing songs (like children's songs) that will help them calm.

The goal is not necessarily to suppress or interrupt the experience but rather to help them explore the experience. Don't try too hard to get them to come down. Do not confuse them with a lot of questions. Avoid complex physical actions. Don't touch them if they do not want to be touched. Give them space and just sit and watch. No pressure.

In exploring ways of changing the setting, take your cues from them. Maybe they want to go to the bathroom.

Maybe they want to put their bare feet on the ground or hug a tree. Try to make eye contact unless they are paranoid or fearful.

Chapter Seven-Entheogens and the Doors of Perception

In the latter part of the twentieth century, the West began to become more aware of various plants that had been used by indigenous cultures to induce or enhance spiritual experiences. But hints and enticing clues to these plants had been noticed much earlier. The Spanish in Mexico and Peru made mention of what they perceived as the demonic practices of the natives in using various substances in their horrible rituals. The Spanish then took the appropriate steps to wipe out the heathen practices – at times in horrible ways. But they recorded little of value about the actual religions and practices of the natives either with or without plants.

The term entheogen refers to a class of plants known variously as hallucinogens, psychedelics and psychotomimetics. They are generally used in traditional cultures along with music, drumming, diet, and ritual to induce altered states of consciousness (ASC) which in turn are used to heal, gain power, and experience visions. They are often used specifically as a means of gaining a spiritual or psychological experience.

It has been hypothesized by some that entheogens played a role in the development of human consciousness and in religious institutions such as shamanism. The origin of the use is lost in prehistory but it may have begun with observation of other animals or through natural experimentation. It is common for animals to experiment with intoxicants (Pollan, 2001, p. 171). Pigeons eating cannabis seeds for example may have been the source of the Scythian discovery of cannabis. Caffeine was discovered after a shepherd saw the excited behavior of goats after eating coffee beans. Some Amazonian Indians have reported that tobacco taught them about Ayahuasca and assumingly the complex process involved in making it. The Tukaro Indians, on the other hand, have a legend that they saw jaguars eating the yage vine and hallucinating and so the reference to "jaguar eyes" in conjunction with ayahuasca use.

Entheogens have long been used ceremonially in state and religious settings. Herodotus reported that the Scythians used cannabis. He also reported that the ancient Persians never made a serious decision without being intoxicated. Rather than Greek propaganda this may have been referring to the use of an entheogen and it is likely that the Persian Homa like the Vedic Soma was just such a visionary substance. Sadhus in India and Sufis in Persia and elsewhere use cannabis and other substances in their spiritual pursuits. Medieval witches allegedly used a combination of Datura, Morning Glories, and Opium Poppies to make their flying ointment. The Eleusian Mysteries which were participated in by Plato, Aristotle, Socrates, Aeschylus, Euripides and other philosophers and poets in ancient Greece, was an ecstatic ritual involving the use of a powerful hallucinogen – possibly ergot though some have wondered about the Amanita muscaria.

There is no single botanical or chemical group for the nearly 100 species of entheogenic plants. The term entheogen refers to their use not to their structure or chemistry (Schultes and Hofmann, 1979). The term hallucinogen, on the other hand, refers to the subjective effects of visions, voices, altered perceptions, and altered mood (Siegel, 1984). An early psychiatric term for these plants was "psychotomimetic" which implies that the experiences have a psychotic basis. The term "psychedelic" means mind-manifesting and was developed mainly in the context of LSD use in the 1960s. Associations of the word "psychedelic" with the counter-culture movement have left it with a negative connotation and so are not generally used to refer to entheogens. Stan Grof (1989), an early researcher in LSD, introduced the term "holotropic" to describe the effects of these substances as seeking wholeness. Shultes and Hofmann (1979) called them "plants of the gods." The term entheogen was introduced by Ruck, Wasson, Staples, Bigwood, and Ott (1979) and derives from the Greek *entheos* meaning the god within, and *gen*, meaning the action of becoming. Michael Winkelman introduced the term "psychointegrator" to reflect their effects on the soul, mind, spirit, and emotions (Winkelman, 1996).

Entheogens have often been repressed by the state and church who have labeled them dangerous, demonic, or both. Some have viewed this repression as a response to a perceived threat to established religious and social power. And, the truth is that entheogens and the altered states of consciousness they bring may present a very real threat to established institutions which rely so heavily on conformity and acceptance of consensual reality and received values (Dobkin de Rios and Smith, 1977).

Entheogens have several positive effects. These include the visions along with psychological and emotional effects which many users report as personally relevant and transformational. Traditional users view entheogens as healing plants and the healing takes place both spiritually and physically. The purgative effect of plants such as Ayahuasca may have been an important defense against worms and other infestation. There is also some evidence that the use of entheogens influences and improves the function of the immune system.

Some have advocated strongly for the use of entheogens and psychedelics as a means of enhancing human life. They have been seen as tools for spiritual improvement as well as important to the further evolution of the human family. Several scientists have considered them to be an important tool for increasing our understanding of human psychology. Terence McKenna, the ethnobotanist, said:

> I often use the metaphor that psychedelics are to psychology what telescopes in the sixteenth century were to astronomy. If a person is not willing to look through the telescope he cannot call himself an astronomer. And if a person is not willing to learn the lessons of the psychedelic compounds, then any therapy he or she does – anything done about the human psyche – is sand-boxed. These are the most powerful agents there are for uncovering the structure and potential of the human mind. (McKenna, 1992, P. 9).

Beginning in the 1960s there have also been a number of studies of the use of entheogens in psychotherapy. Timothy Leary found very positive and long-lasting effects using LSD with prisoners. Walter Pahnke conducted the "Good Friday Experiment" in 1962 with twenty divinity students at the Mersch Chapel at Boston University using psilocybin and a placebo. The result was profound mystical experience and personality change with the psilocybin (Pahnke, 1966). Other researchers including Stanislov Grof experimented with psycholytic psychotherapy by using small doses of LSD in multiple sessions to bring blocked material to consciousness (Grof, 1975/1993, 1980/1994; Passie, 1997). Others including Leary, Grof, and Claudio Naranjo have explored the use of entheogens including LSD and Ayahuasca for therapy with alcoholism and neurosis.

There are clinics and treatment programs that use ayahuasca or other entheogens for the treatment of alcoholism. MDMA has been used in conjunction with psychotherapy and seems to promote self-examination and to decrease fear. It may be useful for those who experience PTSD but has been illegal in therapy in the U.S. since 1985.

Although criticized by some as a trivial experience that does not yield long-lasting effects, the research says otherwise. Emily Laber-Warren reported in *Psychology Today:* "New rigorously designed experiments confirm that while recreational use can be dangerous ...hallucinogens can actually change people for the better – often permanently" (Laber-Warren, 2013, p. 35). Roland Griffiths, professor of Psychiatry and Neuroscience at John Hopkins University, found that after a single dose of psilocybin, nearly two-thirds of thirty-six volunteers reported an increase in their sense of well-being or life satisfaction. In a follow up study more than half of these volunteers scored significantly higher on openness after taking psilocybin. That was a personality change that remained stable fourteen months later. According to Laber-Warren: "Most drugs work only while you're taking them. Psychedelics clear the body within hours, but the effects can last a life-time" (Laber-Warren, 2013, p. 37). Roland Griffiths was equally effusive about this study:

> That first study blew me away,...Nearly all the
> participants reported significant positive changes in
> attitude and behavior, and those changes were
> also observed by the participants' friends, family,
> and colleagues. It was remarkable" (Murphy, 2011,
> p. 34).

Entheogens continue to be used for physical healing and psychological/emotional healing with impressive results. In increasing numbers they are being sought out as sources of spiritual strength and growth with remarkable reports of mystical experiences resulting in profound long-lasting personal change (Griffiths et al, 2011; MacLean et al, 2011). Following we will look at a brief overview of various entheogens.

Mushrooms

Psilocin and psilocybin which breaks down into psilocin in the body are the active agents of ten species of psilocybin mushrooms. The amount of the active agent varies greatly among species but the type having the most constant amounts is Psilocybe semilanceata or Liberty Cap. The main effects, depending on dose, are nausea, facial numbness, and sweating or shivering. It is similar to an LSD trip with vivid and colorful visual effects. It is fairly safe; it would take about eight pounds of fresh mushrooms to overdose. The main danger is that one might pick and eat a poisonous mushroom by mistake.

Psilocin belongs to a family of drugs known as hydroxytriptamines which are largely natural indole drugs. Bufotenine is a close relative found in the skin excretions of some toads and in various trees which grow in Central and South America. One species of toad (bufo alvarius) produces both bufotenine and meo-DMT. A more obscure relative is yohimbe hydrochloride which is found in the bark of Indian and African plants and which is a mild hallucinogen.

The cubensis mushroom (Stropharia cubensis or Psilocybe cubensis) is native to Central and South America and also Southeast Asia. It is known in Latin America as San Isidro. The Hawaiian Copelandia cyanescens or Panaeolus cyanescens is sometimes called "cone-head" or "gold cap" by Hawaiians. Psilocybe Truffles (Psilocybe tampanensis and Psilocybe Mexicana) are sold as "Philosopher's Stone." All of these mushrooms contain the same active agents – psilocin and psilocybin and sometimes baeocystin.

Gordon Wasson was the first to introduce entheogenic mushrooms to the modern Western world. Although a prominent banker he is best known as an ethnomycologist – in fact, the first ethnomycologist. He was led to study with a Mexican shaman, Maria Sabina, and was introduced to the use and ritual surrounding entheogenic mushrooms.

Ayahuasca

It is frequently written that Ayahuasca has been in use in the Amazon Basin for 5000 years although it is not clear how that date has been determined. It was certainly being used when the Spanish arrived in Peru and is mentioned and condemned by some early Spanish writers. In 1851 an English botanist named Richard Spruce collected the first samples of ingredients for making ayahuasca. The drink was observed having divination, healing and psycho-spiritual propensities. (Shultes, Hoffmann, Ratsch, 1992, pp. 124-131). Other intrepid adventurers undoubtedly also encountered entheogens in South America and elsewhere. The adventure writer H. Rider Haggard, the author of *She, King Solomon's Mines,* and many other adventures involving the heroic Allan Quartermain, also mentions entheogens. In *The Ancient Allan* which was published in 1920, and three other novels Haggard writes of an adventure Quartermain had with an African drug called Taduki. As far as I know this is a fictitious drug but entheogenic drugs are used in Africa including the powerful Ibogaine. Early in the adventure however Quartermain meets an adventurer from South America who tells him about yagé, a plant which he says is used in South America for bringing on visions for divination. Yagé is another name still used in parts of South America for ayahuasca. But general knowledge of ayahuasca would have to wait until the middle of the century.

William Burroughs and Allen Ginsberg, iconic figures from the Beat Generation, published the *Yage Letters* in 1964 about their experiences with ayahuasca. Michael Harner, anthropologist and author of *The Shaman's Way*, barely missed the then unknown Ginsberg in Pucallpa, Peru on one of his trips to study Amazonian shamanism. Harner went on to write articles and books regarding ayahuasca. Harner would later serve on the dissertation committee of a Peruvian doctoral student by the name of Carlos Castaneda. Although Castaneda and his books including *The Teachings of Don* Juan have become controversial, he definitely introduced a large audience to the use of entheogens by Native Americans. His books describe, among other things, the use of peyote and datura. Other anthropologists and ethnobotanists including Alberto Villodo and Terence McKenna also studied ayahuasca.

Today ayahuasca has gained the attention of a more general population. In addition to anthropologists and ethnobotanists, it has attracted the attention of others including some celebrities. Celebrities that have used ayahuasca include Paul Simon, Sting, Tori Amos, and Courtenay Love among many others. It has been referred to on television shows including *Weeds, Nip/Tuck,* and the British show *Extreme Celebrity Detox.* It was also very inaccurately portrayed in the movie *Wanderlust* which starred Jennifer Aniston. Aniston, who has no experience with LSD or ayahuasca conflated the two in a way that totally misrepresented a real ayahuasca experience (Phillips, 2014).

Ayahuasca has expanded beyond South America and been the focus of ceremonies in North America, Spain, the Netherlands, and elsewhere including Russia. It has also become the focus of "Ayahuasca tourism" which involves traveling, mostly to Peru, where shamans provide people with an ayahuasca experience that can include weeks in the jungle. Some of these so-called tourists are seeking healing from serious diseases. Others are spiritual seekers. Undoubtedly a few are sensation seeking but the cost of travel and the intensity of the experience probably precludes those who are merely curious.

> Laypeople around the globe have also developed an interest in ayahuasca. While some wish to simply experiment recreationally, most state that their intention is a serious desire to have a spiritual experience of some kind. Travel groups have sprung up around the Amazon at extraordinary rates where tourists can participate in ayahuasca ceremonies most of these travel packages advertise 'native shamans' and an authentic indigenous healing ceremony (Elton 1999). These tours are extremely controversial, with indigenous Amazonians and Western anthropologists as the strongest critics.... (Lewis, P. 111)

Critics of "ayahuasca tourism" accuse those involved of destroying the traditional indigenous practices by their very presence. There may be some truth to this in that some of the tribes or entrepreneurs have created tourist versions to draw in tourist money. Some of these involve the wearing of costumes that have not been worn for over a century and selling tourists authentic trinkets. They may even offer ayahuasca ceremonies given by "shamans" who may or may not follow traditional norms. These are not widespread however and the "blame" lies on both sides. The contrary actually appears to be more likely; ayahuasca tourism is actually contributing to the preservation of traditional ways. It was no doubt a factor in the government of Peru in 2008 declaring ayahuasca to be an official National Treasure. It has also influenced some to stay in their regions and villages to learn the old ways rather than to move to the big city to enter the modern world of Western consumerism.

Critics accuse ayahuasca tourists of consuming scarce resources – which is to say, ayahuasca. Again, the contrary may be more true. Ayahuasca curanderos are generally conservationists and the increased awareness of ayahuasca along with other master plants has increased concern over conservation measures. As mentioned above, ayahuasca itself has been declared a National Treasure. The curanderos take efforts to ensure that ayahuasca and other medicinal plants are harvested in a manner to ensure their future availability.

Criticisms that ayahuasca is bad for the environment seem laughable in the face of the corporate greed that drives so much destruction throughout Amazonia. It also implies that there are huge numbers of ayahuasca tourists streaming into South America when in fact the numbers are comparatively small.

North American visitors to Peru especially are far more likely to visit Machu Picchu and the Incan ruins of the south. Visitors and groups who come year after year to Amazonia are more likely to be Christian missionaries who may do some humanitarian project but who will certainly spread their theology which will include some serious criticism of traditional culture such as the use of ayahuasca. They certainly do much more cultural damage and it could be argued environmental damage as well given the linkage between American culture and Protestant Christian religion. Then there are the sex tourists, especially in Iquitos, usually middle aged men interested in teen-aged girls.

Ayahuasca tourists for the most part are mature adults with an interest in healing or spirituality. Those who are hippies merely interested in another high are relatively few. Of course there are some who are just curiosity or thrill seekers but the nature of ayahuasca and the trappings surrounding it are not encouraging to typical tourists. A typical ayahuasca tour can involve a jungle camp that must be reached by car, canoe and walking. Then there is the shamanic diet which is bland and allows for no condiments or meat. Some come for healing for serious illnesses and others are on a journey of self-discovery. Some stay for years and most have a life-changing experience. Ayahuasca is not a recreational drug and those who seek it out are not the usual tourists. As Adam Elenbaas wrote:

> Having drunk in nearly 25 ayahuasca
> ceremonies with four different shamans from
> three different countries on two different
> continents, I still do not feel capable of defining
> exactly what makes an ayahuasca ceremony
> 'medicine' or 'authentic'. To me, the conversation
> about ayahuasca tourism is usually a cloaked
> conversation about what constitutes a reverent
> psychedelic experience versus a recreational
> experience (Elenbaas, 2013).

Among the more reputable and respected shamans is Don Jose Campos who lives in Pucallpa, Peru. In a country where there are many shamans, Don Jose is widely known and respected among the shamans themselves. He is powerful, energetic and empathic. He is the author of *The Shaman & Ayahuasca* and runs a safe and traditional approach to ayahuasca in his retreat center called Munay (Quechuan for "love"). He also travels frequently to perform ayahuasca ceremonies elsewhere. He is an accomplished musician and frequently enhances his ceremonies with the music of Arturo Mena who like Don Jose is an incredible musician and the grandson of a shaman. I would recommend Don Jose to anyone who is interested in experiencing ayahuasca. (I have no investment or financial interest in Don Jose or his operations.)

Ayahuasca is used traditionally for divination, healing, and for its psycho-spiritual properties. Early anthropologists and ethnobotanists such as Schultes recognized the power of ayahuasca (Shultes, Hofmann and Ratsch, 1992). Among its more notable effects is a sense of unitive consciousness. This is the experience, frequently reported by mystics, that everything is connected.

Many of those who use ayahuasca experience profound visions and most of those I have personally interviewed report the experience as personally important and transformative. Although experiences of struggle and difficulty are frequently reported, they are perceived as significant ordeals or as catharsis.

Ayahuasca is made from the ayahuasca vine (Banisteriopsis caapi) and the leaves of the chakruna plant (Psychotria viridis). Chakruna contains dimethyltryptamine (DMT) but when DMT is taken orally it is inactivated by peripheral monamine oxidase-A (MAO) which is found in the stomach. The function of MAO is to oxidize moleculres which contain an NH2 amine group such as DMT. To allow the DMT to act it is combined with an MAO inhibitor. The ayahuasca vine contain beta-carbolines such as harmine, harmaline, and tetrahydroharmine which inhibit MAO-A. The process of creating the ayahuasca "tea" is labor intense and requires several days. Ayahuasca is not toxic but it is a purgative and the experience of taking it can be uncomfortable. The purgative and emetic effects of Ayahuasca come from the beta-carboline MAO inhibitors which are also responsible for releasing the visions of Chakruna.

DMT can also be ingested by using a route other than the digestive tract such as smoking, injection, or inhalation which bypasses the MAO in the stomach lining. Some of the indigenous people around the Orinoco Basin in Venezuela inhale a snuff called *epana* made from the resinous fluid in the inner bark of several tress of the genus Virola that contain large amounts of DMT (Schultes, 1954; Seit, 1967; Schultes & Swain, 1976). The Guahibo Indians of the Orinoco Basin use a snuff called *yopo* which is made from the DMT-rich beans of the Anadenanthera peregrine plant (De Budowski, Marini-Bettolo, Delle Monache, and Ferrari, 1974; McKenna and Towers, 1985; Ott, 1996).

Mescaline: Peyote and San Pedro

Mescaline has been consumed in its natural form in cacti for possibly thousands of years. In its natural form it is contained in peyote and San Pedro. It was made synthetically in 1919. Its chemical name is trimethoxyphenethylamine which makes it a natural relative to MDMA (ecstasy). The effects of the synthetic drug are different from those of peyote or San Pedro mainly because when people eat the cactus, they are also ingesting around thirty related compounds. Main effects include a dreamy, relaxed state with a peak phase similar to LSD. Various visions may occur including the cactus spirit, Mescalito.

Peyote was long used by Native Americans in what is now south Texas and northern Mexico. It comes from a cactus which is native to that region where it has been used for thousands of years. Petroglyphs in the Big Bend area of the Rio Grande show clear evidence of its use. Carlos Castaneda wrote of its contemporary use in northern Mexico in *The Teachings of Don Juan*. The Mescalero Apaches take their name from the plant whose active agent is mescaline. The Navajo Indians and other tribes of New Mexico adopted its use and it spread from there to the Plains Indians including the Comanche. The famous chief Quanah Parker adopted and advocated its use after his surrender and settlement on a reservation in Oklahoma. It even received the early attention of some psychologists including Joseph Smith III, a psychologist and the son and heir-presumptive of the Mormon Prophet Joseph Smith. Currently peyote is used and recognized for legal use as a sacrament by the Native American Church.

The peyote cactus was first methodically studied by Louis Lewin in 1888. Mescaline, the active agent, was first identified by Karl Wilhelm Hefter, a German pharmacologist. Very early experiments were conducted by the prominent psychologist Havelock Ellis. Humphrey Osmond, who coined the term "psychedelic" in a letter to Aldous Huxley, also introduced Huxley to mescaline in 1953. His experiences with mescaline led to his book – *Doors to Perception* in 1954.

Other natural sources of mescaline include the San Pedro cactus (Trichocereus pachanoi) which Peruvian shamans call *wachuma,* and the Peruvian Torch (Trichocereus peruvianus).

Among the many who have been influenced by mescaline, peyote, and San Pedro was Sartre. Grof observes: "It is worth mentioning that an important influence in Sartre's life was a difficult and poorly resolved session with the psychedelic substance mescaline, the active alkaloid from the Mexican cactus peyote used as a sacrament by the native people" (Grof, 1990, p. 50).

Cannabis

Cannabis may be the oldest of all entheogenic plants. Herodotus described how the ancient Iranian nomads known as Scythians used it over 2500 years ago. It was one of the earliest plants to be cultivated. Among the mummies discovered in the Tarim Basin is one of a shaman who was buried with cannabis (Coppens, 2013). It has such low toxicity that there are no known deaths from overdose.

Pope Innocent VIII condemned cannabis as part of his condemnation of witchcraft in 1484. And though this may seem strange at first, Paracelsus often said he learned everything he knew of medicine from the sorceresses. Charles Baudelaire wrote *Artificiel Paradises* in 1860 concerning hashish.

In the mid-1960s Raphael Mechoulan, an Israeli neuroscientist, identified the active agent of cannabis as delta-9-tetrahydrocannabinol or THC. In 1992, Mechoulen and William Devane discovered that the human body produces its own cannabinoid. They named this endo-genous cannabinoid – anandamide from the Sanskrit word for inner bliss. In 1998 Allyn Howlett of St. Louis University Medical School discovered a specific receptor for THC. There are a large number of cannabinoid receptors found throughout the brain. They tend to cluster in the cortex, hippocampus, basal ganglia and amygdala but not in the brain stem. Receptors for anadamide have also been found in the uterus. It may play a role in helping us to forget pain and according to researchers, in addition to pain management, it may play a role in multiple processes involving appetite and it may even have antibiotic properties.

Andrew Weil has described cannabis as "an active placebo" that does not create the high but instead triggers the high. It is certainly true that the range of effects is quite large. In the 1930s marijuana was associated with violence. But prior to that in the late 19th and early 20th century it was treated as a panacea and used as an ingredient in many medications. More recently indolence has been considered to be a major effect. For Fitzhugh Ludlow and Aleister Crowley it was a potent hallucinogen.

Top quality sinsemilla has sold for $500 or more an ounce and cannabis may be America's leading cash crop. It is certainly the most expensive flower in the world. Until the mid 1970s most marijuana used in the United States was grown in Mexico. Then the U.S. government requested Mexico to spray the crop with the herbicide paraquat and the U.S. began to more vigorously crack down on pot smugglers. Ultimately this led to the increase of the U.S. domestic crop which was initially inferior. American hippies traveling the "hashish trail" through Afghanistan returned with seeds from Cannabis indica which were crossed with Cannabis sativa in America. Sativa grows to 15 feet and Indica to 4 or 5 feet. It was hybridized in California and the Pacific Northwest and the cross-breeding allowed growers in all fifty states to cultivate more potency. Until the 1980s almost all marijuana was grown outdoors. In 1982 the Reagan administration was chagrined with the discovery that the amount of domestic marijuana being seized was actually 1/3 more than the official estimate of the total American crop. The Armed Forces was assigned to the Drug War and growers moved indoors. Moving the hybridized Cannabis to indoor conditions began in the early 1980s in the Pacific Northwest and resulted in a very small plant with much larger flowers and a THC content of around 15%. Ordinary, non-hybridized cannabis was 2-3%. The THC levels today at times reach 20%.

Other sources of non-ordinary states of consciousness and spiritual experience

There are a number of names to describe non-ordinary states of consciousness. These include psychedelic, trance, unitive, mystical, altered, holographic, and shamanic. Each of these terms has strengths and weaknesses along with advocates and critics. The large number of terms reflects various approaches to such states as well as the great variety of sources for non-ordinary states of consciousness. A Benedictine monk may have an ecstatic experience from silent meditation that is similar to that of a Tibetan Buddhist, a natural mystic, or an Amazonian shaman but each will have different names, perceptions, and explanations for the experience.

The problem with many of the terms is that they are tainted by the recreational drug culture of the 1960s – e.g. psychedelic, getting high – or by the materialistic world of disease-focused medicine which is tied closely to the War on Drugs mentality.   But, they are useful in different contexts.

In addition to drugs there are other ways of inducing altered states of consciousness. These include sensory deprivation in a flotation tank or on a vision quest in a dark cavern. Some Native American tribes underwent ordeals through vision quests and in sweat lodges. Consciousness can also be altered through hyperventilating or by spinning as children and Sufis sometimes do. The methods are so varied and the seeking of altered states is so common that Andrew Weil considers it to be a universal characteristic of humans.

There are also spontaneous altered states of consciousness. Some of these may come after many years or months of a spiritual discipline. Others may occur from no apparent trigger as a mystical experience or an ecstatic experience on seeing a wonderful sunset or one's newborn child. Others may appear from some sort of ordeal such as fasting or isolation. These spontaneous altered states may serve some sort of healing or transformative role in human beings. As Stanislav Grof has written:

> The basic idea that there exist spontaneous non-ordinary states that would in the west be seen and treated as psychosis, treated mostly by suppressive medication. But if we use the observation from the study of non-ordinary states, and also from other spiritual traditions, they should really be treated as crises of transformation, or crises of spiritual opening. Something that should really be supported rather than suppressed. If properly understood and properly supported, they are actually conducive to healing and transformation (Redwood and Grof).

216

In reference to spiritual emergencies another useful but lengthy term is used by Mario Beauregard and Denyse O'Leary in *The Spiritual Brain.* That term is Religious, Spiritual, or Mystical Experiences or RSMEs. This term is broad enough to include such as things as Near Death Experiences, induced states, and responses to profound life changes, as well as states induced by entheogenic plants, meditation, breathing, or sensory deprivation. It has the advantage for our purposes of focusing on spiritual experiences as opposed to intoxication or visual effects.

Many RSMEs occur in the context of religious beliefs and activities. These may be described in various ways depending on the religious context. An evangelical Christian might be born again while someone in another context might be enlightened, inspired, called, touched by the spirit, experience kundalini rising, have a revelation, see an angel, hear the voice of God, or have a spontaneous mystical experience. Evelyn Underhill, the great scholar of mysticism, observed: "Almost any religious system which fosters unearthly love is potentially a nursery for mystics" (Underhill, 1974, p. 96).

The prevalence of RSMEs in religious contexts has led some to suppose that RSMEs derive from religions. This creates an unfortunate perception that the RSME of one religion is somehow qualitatively different from that of another which does not seem to be the case. Also, it assumes that from an evolutionary perspective religion came first and was followed later by the appearance of spirituality. As others have observed: "... there is a serious weakness to this approach to explaining RSMEs. To study mysticism or spirituality as if it derives from religion is to reverse the usual course of events" (Beauregard and O'Leary, p. 209). Some scholars, including Terence

217

McKenna, have proposed that RSMEs induced by the use of entheogenic plants led to the development of spirituality among prehistoric humans.

The religious scholar, Rudolf Otto (1869-1937) coined the term "numinous" to describe that sense of awe and wonder some feel in the presence of the holy. This provides some insight into RSMEs and the subjective experience felt in such cases. Dr. Herbert Benson of the Harvard Medical School and researcher in mind/body medicine also views certain spiritual experiences as a natural and intrinsic part of the human experience:

> Our bodies are wired to benefit from exercising not only our muscles but our rich inner, human core— our beliefs, values, thoughts, and feelings. I was reluctant to explore these factors because philosophers and scientists have, through the ages, considered them intangible and immeasurable, making any study of them 'unscientific.' But I wanted to try, because, again and again, my patients' progress and recoveries often seemed to hinge upon their spirit and will to live. And I could not shake the sense I had that the human mind— and the beliefs we so often associate with the human soul-had physical manifestations (Benson and Stark, 1996, p. 17).

To put it another way, RSMEs can be extremely beneficial to human beings. They are not evidence of pathology or brain dysfunction. In fact, people who report having RSMEs score lower on measures of psychopathology and higher on measures of psychological well-being than those who do not report such experiences (Beauregard and Targ, p. 291). In fact the positive changes which occur in those who experience RSMEs is long-lasting as noted by Beauregard and Targ:

The psychospiritual transformation that often follows RSMEs can involve changes in thoughts, emotions, attitudes, core beliefs about self and the world, and behaviors. Maslow's work and that of other pioneers such as James and Hardy has shown that RSMEs are commonly associated with a transcendence of the personal identity and an enhanced sense of connection to and unity with others and the world. This process of self-transcendence awakens one to one's transcendental or spiritual self. It is noteworthy that similar changes are frequently seen in NDErs following their NDEs. Thus, spiritual values of love and compassion for oneself, others, and nature and acquiring knowledge about the divine often become much more important after NDEs, whereas such values as wealth, status, and material possessions become much less important. (Beauregard and Targ, p. 291).

The effects of RSMEs are, in short, not trivial, superficial, or pathological. They are rather transformative and profound. Reports from people who have experienced RSMEs almost always reveal profound effects that transform the person's life. These are transcendent experiences. Brain dysfunction, on the other hand, produces trivial experiences that are neither transformative or positive. Beauregard and Targ have commented on the positive effects of RSMEs:

There is no scientific evidence showing that delusions or hallucinations produced by a dysfunctional brain can induce the kind of long-term positive changes and psychospiritual transformation that often follow RSMEs. In fact, delusions and hallucinations usually constitute

219

negative experiences from a subjective
perspective. (Beauregard and Targ, p. 292)

Other researchers have also observed the positive
aspects of such effects and the clear difference between
them and pathological conditions:

We do not believe that genuine mystical
experiences can be explained away as the results of
epileptic hallucinations or, for that matter, as the
product of other spontaneous hallucinatory states
triggered by drugs, illness, physical exhaustion,
emotional stress, or sensory deprivation.
Hallucinations, no matter what their source, are
simply not capable of providing the mind with
an experience as convincing as that of mystical
spirituality (Newberg, et al, 2001, p. 111).

Even the manner in which such experiences are
stored and recalled differs notably from the perception
and recall of pathological experiences. These
transpersonal experiences are indicative of healthier
minds and the neurological correlates coincide with what
researchers, such as Maslow, have called "peak
experiences" or "transcendent experiences":

After years of research...our understanding of
various key brain structures and the way
information is channeled along neural pathways
led us to hypothesize that the brain possesses a
neurological mechanism for self-transcendence.
The mind remembers mystical experience with the
same degree of clarity and sense of reality that it
bestows upon memories of 'real' past events. The
same cannot be said of hallucinations, delusions, or

dreams. We believe this sense of realness strongly suggests that the accounts of the mystics are not indications of minds in disarray, but are the proper, predictable neurological result of a stable, oherent mind willing itself toward a higher spiritual plane. (Newberg, et al, 2001, pp. 145-146, 113)

Entheogenic Therapy

The effects of entheogens are similar to those of awakened Kundalini (DeGracia, 2013). Not surprisingly they have played and continue to play a role in various religious and spiritual traditions. Well-known entheogens include peyote, ayahuasca, the San Pedro Cactus, psilocybin mushrooms, and cannabis. Tobacco has been used as a sacred plant in various forms by the native people of the western hemisphere. It continues to be used in pipe ceremonies and other sacred ceremonies. It is also used therapeutically and for cleansing and protection among the Shipibo people of the Ucayali River region in Peru and presumably elsewhere in South America (Wilbert, 1987, p. 93).

It is likely that knowledge of medicinal plants preceded the development of agriculture. Even today much of the western pharmacopeia is derived from plants. Pseudoephedrine is derived from ephedra plant species. Taxol, a medication used in cancer treatment, is derived from an alkaloid found in the Yew tree. Quinine is an anti-malarial medication derived from the bark of the Cinchona tree and first used by Quechuan speaking natives of Amazonia. And this is but a small sampling.

Since at least the 1960s various entheogens have been considered for use in psychotherapy. In 1962 Sherwood and his colleagues published "The Psychedelic

Experience—A New Concept in Psychotherapy" in which they noted:

> LSD in particular, has been used in contemporary psychotherapy, most often as an adjunct to conventional therapeutic procedures. The therapeutic results with these materials are dependent not only upon dosage, but upon the intention of the subject as he submits himself to the experience, the kind of preparation he has had prior to the taking of the material, the setting of the session, and the help of a therapist who has himself explored deeply in these unfamiliar regions of the mind (Sherwood, et al., 1962, p. 69).

This is in harmony with traditional uses where entheogens are used to help people emotionally and spiritually as well as physically. Although altered states of consciousness such as those experienced with entheogens are not usually associated with healing and therapy in the West where the "war on drugs" mentality prevails, they have been an important tool for healers and helpers throughout human history and presumably prehistory. Ludwig wrote: "The induction of these states has been employed for almost every conceivable aspect of psychological therapy" (Ludwig, p. 19).

LSD was used successfully by Timothy Leary in the rehabilitation of prisoners (Leary, 1969). Positive effects using psychedelic drugs have also been found in the treatment of alcohol abuse and depression. Psycholytic (soul-dissolving, mind-loosening) doses which are lower than psychedelic doses of MDMA and LSD have been used in psychotherapy.

The general approach to entheogens in therapy has been similar to their use in traditional societies. They are not used as medications to treat certain symptoms nor are they seen as a cure in and of themselves. Rather they are seen as a means of access to the underlying energy and wisdom. As Sherwood described the process:

> The concept underlying this approach is that an individual can have a single experience which is so profound and impressive that his life experience in the months and years that follow become a continuing growth process (Sherwood, et. al., 1962, p. 69).

Ironically although entheogens have been condemned in the war on drugs, they have been used successfully in the treatment of drug addiction and abuse. LSD was studied in the 1950s as a treatment for alcoholism and drug addiction (Abramson 1967; Grof 1980; Bliss 1988). Other hallucinogens such as ketamine (Krupitsky et al 1992) and ibogaine (Mash et al 2000) have been studied in the treatment of addictions. Much of the Western research on the use of ayahuasca in psychotherapy has been focused on the treatment of addiction (Winkelman, 2001; Grob, 1994, p. 111). Hallucinogenic mushrooms have been found to have long lasting benefits including increased openness and receptiveness to new ideas (Frood, 2008; McGreal, 2012).

There is also evidence that the use of entheogens may be useful for overall health. The natives of Amazonia have used ayahuasca and other medicinal plants for thousands of years for healing physical ailments. The purging that often accompanies the use of ayahuasca has been hypothesized as healthy in an environment where parasites are a common problem – as in Amazonia. There is also evidence of entheogen-induced mystical experiences boosting the immune system as measured by levels of salivary immunoglobulin A (Roberts, 1999).

Of course some caution must be taken to avoid simply introducing entheogenic plants into the Western materia medica as another allopathic medication. In the Western medical model, doctors diagnose and find a disease which they then treat by cutting it out, radiating it, or medicating it. In traditional societies where entheogenic plants and other healing plants have been used for thousands of years a different pattern is used. If a person seeks healing the shaman or curandero may seek information through divination. This could involve some sort of communication with spirits or other divination including taking an entheogenic plant. This might reveal the source of the problem which the shaman will treat as directed by the spirits with other healing plants or by having the person take an entheogenic plant.

The plant is used in a ceremony – a ritual that involves invoking the spirit of the plant through the singing of songs or chanting. Other rituals may be involved in the preparation of the plant and other aspects of the process. Those who participate hold an intention for the ceremony and depending on the culture there may be prayer, communal singing, flower baths, sweat lodges, and other rituals.

A major point of difference is that when Western therapists use entheogenic plants or psychedelic drugs, the plants are often treated as allopathic medications. That is to say, the therapist has the patient take the medication while the therapist watches or perhaps tries to guide the process. Another danger is that Big Pharma will take the plants and reduce them to one or two alkaloids. The people would then be deprived not just of a cultural setting and its ritual but also of the total mixture of alkaloids available from any given medicinal plant. In traditional societies the shaman or curandero takes the medicinal plant along with the people he is trying to help. Sometimes the shaman takes medicine plant himself and learns how to help the person. The shaman holds the space energetically for the ceremony but each person in the ceremony undergoes their own process. After the process, there is no process group (although there is sometimes a little check in group for Westerners). Each person is encouraged to process individually in order to integrate the experience.

Another danger is that Big Pharma will take the plants and reduce them to one or two alkaloids. People would then be deprived not just of a cultural setting and its ritual but also of the total mixture of alkaloids available from any given medicinal plant. The complexity of the sacred would be reduced to the artificial simplicity of the marketable and profitable.

Integration and Grounding

Talking is not the same thing as integrating. Unfortunately for Westerners, talking is central to every type of experience whether profound or mundane. I have observed that many of those who are involved in the ayahuasca experience encourage pre-ayahuasca groups to talk about what they are going to experience and post-groups for talking about what they experienced. This is not of course the traditional approach to ayahuasca or other entheogens where the encounter with the plant medicine is the most important thing. Even today although curanderos tend to go along with the Western need to process and talk, it is clear that they perceive the entheogen itself as the central part – in fact the only part of the experience that matters. I heard the prominent curandero, Don Jose Campos, say that although there are many books available to read about ayahuasca, the only way to really learn about ayahuasca is to take it. On the other hand, Don Jose and other curanderos encourage people to spend time alone – thinking and processing about their experience. They also encourage adherence to the traditional *dieta* with the idea that it will help with the integration and changes that the plant offers. Following are some other ideas to help with integration and grounding.

When experiencing the unitive experience, people become aware of the interconnectedness of all things and all beings. This leads to an awareness of the immanence of the Divine. In other words, everything is sacred and everything including ourselves is an aspect of the Divine. This realization leads some to a personal awareness of their own divinity – e.g. "I am god." This awareness has been expressed many times by the great mystics of history and unfortunately led to the martyrdom or hospitalization of many enlightened souls. If experiencing or helping someone with this experience, remember that "I am god" is not the same thing as being right, better, infallible, omniscient, or omnipotent. Such a unitive experience is a process of joining in a universal way of being, feeling, and thinking about the world. That is different from joining a group of believers whose allegiance is to an institution or creed.

Integration following the use of entheogens is for the most part a natural process. In traditional societies where entheogens are used they are usually viewed as central sources of spiritual experience and religious participation. This led Shultes and Hofmann (1979) to refer to them as "plants of the gods". One researcher has referred to them as psychointegrators which "implies stimulation of mind, emotions, soul and spirit to integrative development" (Winkelman, 2003). Entheogens stimulate integration of the brain's behavioral and social-emotional processing output to produce theta wave links between the limbic or emotional system and the behavioral brain to send ascending impulses to the frontal cortex. This may produce repressed memories, integration of emotional and rational processes and the resolution of conflicts through the integration of various functions. It is, in other words, a systemic and a psycho-social integration (Winkelman, 2003).

Intention is crucial for integration. Before you partake in an entheogen, form an intention. It need not be specific but can be as simple as focusing on growth, healing, becoming a better helper, becoming more spiritual or any desire or question you might have. If your intention is integration and growth, then hold that intention. Regardless of the discipline or path you choose be careful about your intentions. Avoid making phenomena such as visions your goal. Although such "special effects" can be helpful and interesting, the ultimate purpose of spiritual disciplines transcends entertainment. In other words, hold an intention but do not be invested in the form in which it manifests. That is good advice in general for life. Develop an intention but do not become attached to an outcome. Outcomes are often outside our control but intentions reflect our inner state and so lie completely within our control.

Focus instead on how you can use the new knowledge and energy you gain from such experiences. Pray, send silent blessings and compassion to others, and allow your experience to lead to creativity. And, most importantly, avoid self-judgment. Instead of judging yourself as "weird" or "losing it" recognize that you are "special" and "blessed".

Bring the spiritual down to earth. This is the process we call grounding. This involves working with your thoughts. It is not necessary for you to process or understand the experience immediately or all at once. It is a process. Rest your mind. In order to assimilate markedly new things confusion is a necessary part of the process. There is no need to fight it.

Instead of trying constantly to understand or interpret these profound experiences simply practice gratitude. Instead of struggling with understanding and possibly yielding to frustration or even fear, just recognize the abundance of blessings that have come your way. Say prayers of thanksgiving. Keep a gratitude journal. Such disciplines will help you shift from mentally over-processing to a more open-hearted, peaceful assimilation of the experience.

Grounding is to a great extent a matter of paying attention to your body. Unfortunately modern society has trained us to ignore the body. When we experience intense feelings, whether good or bad, we are trained to shut down. This disconnect creates problems at multiple levels for individuals and the society at large. The sudden occurrence of intense feelings, especially when left uninterpreted, can lead to feeling or fearing a loss of control. Simply notice what you are feeling in your body without resistance. It is the difference between standing rigidly while a wave crashes into you and going soft and flexible to ride the wave. Resistance leads to battering while flexibility leads to greater energy.

Much of integration deals with dealing with our ego and issues related to the ego. We all have one and with our ego we also have all the fears and flaws that attend human existence. To rise above ego issues does not mean that we deny them or ignore them. It does not require struggle. It means allowing ourselves to accept and transcend the judgment, drama, and investment in the ego. As we approach this level we are approaching real spiritual power even if it is not accompanied by dramatic spiritual phenomena (what some call "special effects").

From my personal experiences and through my conversations with other psychonauts it seems that entheogens like ayahuasca seem to be aimed at communicating at a level beyond language. These types of experiences are by definition – ineffable and yet so many westerners seem intent on reducing them to everyday speech (what we might call "effing the ineffable"). Avoid that temptation. Rather than endless talk about your journeys and visions just quietly meditate on them. Rather than trying to reduce them to an intellectual process, allow yourself to feel them emotionally and somatically.

The best indicator of a spiritual life is our love. Love of God, love of other living beings, love of self, love of all creation creates a much more meaningful context for our spiritual experiences than do spiritual adventures. It is much easier to maintain our center and groundedness when focused on love than when we are listening to the ego.

The truth is that integration or even simply experiencing profound spiritual experiences can cause a reflexive resistance. How could it be otherwise? It can be a surge of power. It can turn one's long-held beliefs and perceptions upside down. Relax, breath and simply let yourself go into the experience. At times you can check in by asking yourself if you are taking care of essentials like your job, your family, and the daily tasks of living. We can be led or called to some important spiritual mission but if we are unable to take care of the basic tasks required of being in the world then we probably are not going to be able to do the sacred work either. Slow the process down. This is especially important if considering major changes such as career changes, divorce, and so on.

Conclusion: Where to go from here

It has become fashionable to use the word "holistic" to describe a variety of services but calling something "holistic" does not make it so. The word comes from an Old English word and is cognate with the words "whole" and "health". The idea behind the word is that we can increase our health by attending to our wholeness. Allopathic medical clinics and physicians who tout a holistic medical practice are essentially oxymoronic since they focus solely on the biological and omit large segments of the human experience such as spirituality, nutrition, and even social and physical activity. Some even ignore emotional and mental experience as at best secondary and at worst irrelevant to their practice. Psychotherapists and counselors cannot afford to quietly accept this approach.

A truly holistic approach to health, therapy, or any type of helping profession requires a sort of rigor that is not seen often in today's society. It requires us to make an honest personal inventory and best effort toward our own health and wholeness. In order to provide others with the optimal help, we must be personally prepared. That requires a dedication toward lifelong learning and perfecting the skills of our trade. A mastery of the basics and internalization of the principles of helping is essential and does not come just from a degree or a weekend seminar.

We must also attempt to model healthy behaviors and choices in our own lives. Too often there is a tendency among some would-be helpers to judge and to hold clients to a higher standard then they hold themselves. Consider the message that is sent by an overweight counselor who eats poorly, never exercises, and has a limited or non-existent social, spiritual, or intellectual life outside the workplace. Consider personally what it means to be a therapist whose life is plagued by physical and emotional aches and pains.

The well-known myth of the wounded healer is often distorted into the idea that therapists and counselors chose their field in order to deal with their own issues. It is sometimes said that a person has to have a lot of problems in order to be a shrink. In the original concept the healer is not required to be wounded bur rather to be healed. It should be called the myth of the healed healer. In other words, the true healers undergo trials, experiences, and initiations that have increased their understanding, wisdom, empathy, and ability to help others.

So, what to do? Here are some suggestions that might help us increase our ability to provide holistic services to help others:

- Keep on learning. This entails reading and studying not just the new research and information but also the classics in your field. Also be open to learning about lots of things. The more we learn the more effective we become at understanding the world and in connecting with others.
- Learning is not confined to reading. Of course we can take classes, watch DVDs and

attend conferences but we can also learn by experience. Make a point of learning new skills. These could be anything – mechanics, carpentry, tatting, mountaineering, skiing, yoga, sushi making. There is no wasted learning.

- Attend to your fitness by moving your body regularly. Go to the gym, exercise at home, do yoga, qigong, play ping pong, run. Holistic means body-mind-spirit. You will feel better, have more energy, and will function better. And when you encourage a sedentary client to exercise, you will speak with the authority of experience.

- You are what you eat so pay attention to nutrition. On the one hand, that means to avoid fats, white carbs including refined sugar, processed foods and especially fast foods. More specifically I recommend that you consider becoming a vegetarian or a vegan. If you are what you eat, then do you really want to eat the corpses of tortured sentient beings who have been pumped full of antibiotics and chemicals. Read *The China Study* by Campbell and see the DVD *Forks over Knives*.

- Get a life. We are all multifaceted and that means we all need to have a variety of interests and activities. Social activities are an important part of our humanity and our wholeness. Make connections and enjoy them. Vary your activities. This is an important part of staying flexible and growing.

- Remember that what we focus on tends to be what we get. So focus on the things you want to manifest in your life. Develop a positive, optimistic approach to life.
- Meditate. This is a major tool for both our mental and spiritual health. Spend some time daily in some sort of meditation that will help to quiet the monkey-cage that we call our mind. There are many approaches to meditation but the specific approach is not as important as the consistency.
- Pray. Although similar to meditation prayer goes beyond mind discipline to connection with the Divine (or whatever name you use for the Transcendent). To a great extent prayer is an exercise in gratitude. Express your gratitude before meals and other scheduled times. Meister Eckhardt said: "If the only prayer you said in life was 'Thank you,' that would suffice."
- Read devotional and inspirational material. This could be scriptures or other materials including poetry. Read them. Contemplate on them and even memorize some.
- Get out in Nature. Live the connection that we feel in mystical and ecstatic. experiences. Observe and enjoy the sights, sounds, smells and other sensations.
- Practice your religion or spirituality. It is not just an intellectual exercise nor is it merely about beliefs and doctrines. There is great benefit from rituals and communal activities. There is an even greater benefit in applying such principles as compassion,

love, hope, empathy, faith, kindness, and charity in everyday life. Meister Eckhardt said: "That which is taken in by inspiration must be given out through love."

These recommendations for developing a holistic approach to your practice as a therapist, counselor or other helping professional are really methods of integrating the lessons of religious, spiritual, and mystical experiences. Simply talking about your latest reading, ritual, yoga practice, ayahuasca vision, sound healing, or meditation does not bring the lesson home. The ultimate integration is the implementation of the lessons in your daily life to improve your life and reaffirm the connection with the divine energy. The key is persistence and consistency and to these I would add dancing, singing, and laughter.

Blessings and good journey.

Bibliography

Abramson, H. (1967) Use of LSD in Psychotherapy and Alcoholism.
New York: Bobbs-Merrill.

Adams, Celeste. (2001). Help for People in Spiritual Crisis with Karen
Trueheart. Spirit of Ma'at Vol. 2 Number 2.
www.spiritofmaat.com/archives/sep2/prns/trueheart.htm.
Accessed 3//17/2014.

Allman, L.S., De La roche, O., Elkins, D.N., and Weathers, R.S. (1992).
Psychotherapists' attitudes towards clients reporting mystical
experiences. *Psychotherapy, 29,* 564-569.

American Counseling Association (2014). *Code of Ethics.*

American Psychological Association (2002). *Ethics Code.*

Anderson, R.G. and Young, J.L. (1988)

Anderson, Douglas A. and Worthen, Dan. (1997, Jan). Exploring A
Fourth Dimension: Spirituality As A Resource For the Couple
Therapist. *Journal of Marital and Family Therapy* VOl. 23,
Issue 1, pp. 3-12.

Aguilera, D. (1998). *Crisis Intervention: Theory and methodology.* St.
Louis, MO: Mosby.

Assagioli, R. (1989). Self-realization and psychological disturbance. In
Grof & Grof (1989).

Assagioli, R. (2014). Transpersonal development, Crisis of the spiritual
development. Psychonautdocs. com/docs /Assagioli
_transpersonal.htm. Accessed 5/29/2014.

Basedow, H. (1925). *The Australian Aboriginal.* Adelaide: F.W. Preece.
Quoted in W.B. Cannon (1942)

Beauregard, Mario and Denyse O'Leary. The Spiritual Brain: A
Neuroscientist's Case For The Existence Of The Soul.
HarperOne: New York, 2007

Begley, Elizabeth and Ann Leonard. (1992). "How Wild Animals Use
Nature's Medicine Chest". *Newsweek
(February 3, 1992).*

Benson, Herbert, and Marg Stark. (1996). Timeless Medicine: the

Power and Biology of Belief. New York: Scribner

Bergin, A. (1980). Psychotherapy and Religious Values. *American Psychologist*, 48, 1980, 95-105.

Bergin, A. and Jensen, J. (1990). Religiosity of psychotherapists: A national survey. *Psychotherapy*, 27, 3-7.

Bergin, Allen. In Jeff Levin and Harold G. Koenig, eds. *Faith, Medicine, and Science: A Festscrift in Honor of Dr. David B. Larson*. New York: Haworth, 2005.

Berkman, L.F., & Syme, S.L. (1979). Social networks, host resistance, and mortality: A nine-year follow-up study of Alameda County residents. *American Journal of Epidemiology*, 109: 186-204.

Bertini, M., Lewis, H. and Witkin, H. "Some preliminary observation with an experimental procedure for the study of hypnagogic and similar phenomena," *Archivio de Psicologia, Neurologia, Psichiatria e Psicoterapia* 25 (1964): 493-534.

Bliss, K. (1988) LSD and Psychotherapy. Contemporary Drug Problems 15(4): 519-563.

Bock, P.K. (1999) *Rethinking Psychological Anthropology: Continuity and Change in the Study of Human Action*, 2d edition. Prospect Heights, IL: Waveland Press.

Bogart, G. (1991). The use of meditation in psychotherapy. *American Journal of Psychotherapy*, 45 (3), 383-412.

Bonelli, Raphael; Dew, Rachel E.; Koenig, Harold G.; Rosmarin, David H.; and Vasegh, Sasan. (2012) Religious and Spiritual Factors in Depression: Review and Integration of the Research. Depression Research and Treatment, Vol. 2012 (2012), Article ID 962860. http://dx.doi.org/10.1155/2012/962860

Bragdon, E. (1993). *A sourcebook for helping people with spiritual problems*. Apo, CA: Lightening Up Press.

Breggin, Peter and Cohen, David. (1999). *Your Drug May Be Your Problem: How and Why to Stop Taking Psychiatric Medications.* Da Capo Press: Philadellphia, PA

Burroughs, William S. & Ginsberg, Allen. *The Yage Letters.* San Francisco: City Lights Books, 1963.

Callaway, J.C., D.J. McKenna, C.S. Grob, G.S. Brito, L.P. Raymon, R.E. Poland, E.N. Andrade, E.O. Andrade and D.C. Mash (1999) Pharmacokinetics of *Hoasca* in Healthy Humans. Journal of Ethnopharmacology 65: 243-256.

Cannon, W.B. (1942). "Voodoo" death. *American Anthropologist.* 44: 169-81.

Cannon, W.B. (2002) "Voodoo" death. *American Journal of Public Health* 92:1593-1596.

Caplan, Mariana. (1999). *Halfway Up the Mountain: The Error of Premature Claims of Enlightenment*. Hohm Press: Prescott, Arizona.

Caplan, Mariana (2010) "10 Spiritually Transmitted Diseases" *Huffington Post Healthy Living*. Posted 6/15/10. Accessed 4/3/2014.

Capra, Fritjof. *The Tao of Physics* Boston: Shambhala Publications, 2008

Cashwell, C.S., & Young, J.S. (2011) Integrating spirituality and religion into counseling: A guide to competent practice. Alexandria, VA: American Counseling Association.

Cashwell, C.S., Bentley, P.B., & Yarborough, J.P. (2007). The only way out is through: The peril of spiritual bypass. Counseling and Values, 51, 139-148

Clarke, I. (2001). *Psychosis and spirituality: Explorng a new frontier*. London, England: Whurr Publishers.

Clenmuller, Joseph. *The Antidepressant Solution: A Step-by-Step Guide to Safely Overcoming Antidepressant withdrawal, Dependence and "Addiction"* Free Press: London, 2005

Conway, David. Magic: An Occult Primer (New York: Bantam, 1973 pp. 129-132.

Coppens, P. (2013). *The Lost Civilization Enigma: A New Enquiry into the Existence of Ancient Cities, Cultures, and Peoples Who Pre-date Recorded History*. Paopton Plains, NJ: The Career Press

Crowley, Nicki. (2006). "Psychosis or Spiritual Emergency? – Consideration of the Transpersonal Perspective within Psychiatry." www.rcpsych.ac.uk/pdf/Nicki Crowley. Accessed 3/18/2014.

De Feo, V. (2004) The Ritual Use of *Brugmansia* Species in Traditional Andean Medicine in Northern Peru. Economic Botany 58: 221-229.

Davis, Wade. (1985). *The Serpent and the Rainbow*. Simon and Schuster: New York

Dobkin de Rios, M. (1972) Visionary Vine: Hallucinogenic Healing in the Peruvian Amazon. Prospect Heights, IL: Waveland Press.

Dobkin de Rios, M. (1994) Drug Tourism in the Amazon. Newsletter, Society for the Anthropology of Consciousness 5(1): 16-19. American Anthropological Association.

DeGracia, Donald J. Do Psychedelic Drugs Mimic Awakened Kundalini? Hallucinogen Survey Results. Council on Spiritual Practices. http://csp.org/practices/entheogen/dics.jybdakubu_survey. html. Accessed 4/15/2014.

Douglas-Klutz, N. (2001). Missing stories: Psychosis, spirituality, and the development of Western religious hermeneutics. In I. Clarke (Ed.), *Psychosis and spirituality: Exploring the new frontier* (pp. 53-72). London: Whurr Publishers.

Elenbaas, Adam. Will the Real Ayahuasca Tourists Please Stand Up? Reality Sandwich Magazine. http://www.reality sandwich.com/will_real_ayahuasca_tourists_please_stand. Quoted in Heaven, 2013, Location 1195.

Eliade, M. (1974 [1964]) *Shamanism: Archaic Techniques of Ecstasy*. Princeton, NJ: Princeton University Press.

Ellison, C.G. & George, L.K. (1994). Religious involvement, social ties, and social support in a southeastern community. *Journal for the Scientific Study of Religion* 33: 46-61.

Ellis, A. (1980). "Psychotherapy and atheistic values: A response to A.E Bergin's "Psychotherapy and Religious Issues"." *Journal of Consulting and Clinical Psychology 48: 635-639.*

Elton, C. (1999) Day Trippers. Outside 24 (10): 34

Epstein, M. (1990). Psychodynamics of Meditation: Pitfalls on the Spiritual Path. *Journal of Transpersonal Psychology,* 22(1), 17-34.

Everyly, George S. (2000). "Pastoral Crisis Intervention: Toward a Definition. *International Journal of Emergency Mental Health, 2(2), 69-71.*

Fadiman, James. (2012). *The Psychedelic Explorers' Guide: Safe and Therapeutic and Sacred Journeys*. Rochester, VT:Park Street Press.

Flournoy, Théodore. (1994). *From India to the Planet Mars: A Case of Multiple Personality with Imaginary Languages.* Forward by C.G. Jung. Commentary by Mireille Cifali. Edited and introduction by Sonu Shamdasani. Princeton University Press: Princeton, NJ, 1994.

Flynn, C.P. (1982). Meanings and implications of NDEr ransformations: Some preliminary findings and implications. *Anabiosis*, 1982, 2, 3-14.

Foucault, M. (1967[1961] *Madness and Civilization: A History of Insanity in the Age of Reason*. London: Tavistock.

Fowler, James W. (1981). *Stages of Faith*. Harper and Row: New York.

Frank, Jerome (1961) *Persuasion and Healing: A Comparative Study of Psychotherapy* quoted in Spiritual Competency Resource: Psychic Experiences. www. Spiritualcompetency.com /dsm4/lesson3.6.html   Accessed 3/10/2014.

Frankl, Viktor. (1959) *Man's Search for Meaning*. Boston, MA: Beacon Press

Gallup, G. (1987) *The Gallup Poll: Public Opinion 1986* Wilmington, DE: Scholarly Resources

Gettis, Alan (1978). Psychotherapy as Exorcism. *Journal of Religion and Health*. Vol., 15, No. 3. 188-189.

Gould, Stephen J. (1992). "The Case of the Creeping Fox Terrier Clone." In *Bully For Brontosaurus: Reflections in Natural History*. W.W. Norton: New York: New York. Pp. 155-167.

Greeley, G. (1974). *Ecstasy: A way of knowing*. Englewood Cliffs, NJ: Prentice Hall

Greenstone, J.L., and Leviton, S.C. (2002). *Elements of crisis intervention: Crises and how to respond to them*. Pacific Grove, CA: Brooks/Cole.

Greyson, B. (1983). *Increase in Psychic Phenomena Following Near-Death Experiences*. Theta, volume 11, Number 2, Summer 1983, pp. 26-29

Greyson, B., and Stevenson, I. The phenomenology of near-death experiences. *American Journal of Psychiatry, 1980, 137, 1193-1196.*

Griffiths, R., M. Johnson, W. Richards, B. Richards, U. McCann, and R. Jesse. 2011 "Psilocybin occasioned mystical-type experiences: Immediate and persisting dose-related effects." *Psychopharmacology*. 187 (3): 268-83. DOI: 10.1007/s00213-011-2358-5

Grob, C.S. (1994) Psychiatric Research with Hallucinogens: What have We Learned? In *Yearbook of Ethnomedicine*. C. Ratsch and J. Baker, eds. Pp. 91-112. Berlin: Verlagfyr Wissenschaft und Bildung (VWB).

Grof, S. (1980) The Adventure of Self-Discovery: Dimensions of Consciousness and New Perspectives in Psychotherapy and Inner Explanation. New York: SUNY Press.

Grof, S. and Grof, C. (1986). Spiritual Emergency: The Understanding and Treatment of Transpersonal Crises. ReVision 8 (2), 7-20.

Grof, S. (1987). "Spirituality, Addiction, and Western Science." *Re-Vision Journal* 10:5-18.

Grof, S. and C. Grof (1989) Spiritual Emergency: When Transformation
Becomes a Crisis. New York: Jeremy P. Tarcher/Putnam.

Grof, S. (1990). P. 40) The Holotropic Mind. Harper: San Francisco,
1990, p. 40).

Grof, S. (2008). "Brief History of Transpersonal Psychology"
International Journal of Transpersonal Studies. Vol. 27:
46-54

Grof, S. (2009). Spiritual Emergencies: Understanding and Treatment
of Psychospiritual Crises.
http://realitysandwich.com/1800/spiritual_emergencies/
Accessed 3/7/2014.

Grof, S. and Redwood, D. (1995) Frontiers of the Mind, Interview with
Stanislav Grof, M.D. Health World Online   Belief.net.

Grof, Stanislav. Psychology of the Future_discoveringwisdom.htm
discoveringwisdom.com/2013/03/31/psychology_of_the_fut
ure. Accessed 4/15/2014.

Grosso, M. (1981). Toward an explanation of near-death phenomena.
Journal of the American Society for Psychical Research, 75,
37-60.

Group for the Advancement of Psychiatry. (1976). Mysticism: Spiritual
quest or mental disorder. New York: Group for the
Advancement of Psychiatry.

Gupta, Mahendranath. (1977). The Gospel of Sri Ramakrishna New
York: Ramakrishna-Vivekananda Center

Hardy, Alister. The Spiritual Nature of Man. Oxford: Clarendon, 1979.

Harner, M.J., ed. (1973) Hallucinogens and Shamanism. New York:
Oxford University Press.

Hastings, Arthur. (1983). "A Counseling approach to parapsychological
experience." Journal of Transpersonal Psychology 15(2): 143-
167.

Heaven, Ross. (2013). Ayahuasca: The Vine of Souls. Washington, USA:
Moon Books. (ebook)

Hollis, James. (2005) Finding Meaning in the Second Half of Life: How
to Finally, Really Grow Up.

House, J.S., Landis, K., and Umberson, D. (1988). Social relationships
and health. Science 4965: 540-545.

Hubbard, Marion (2009). So-called 'schizophrenia' as spiritual
emergency. www.scribd.com/doc/.../Socalled-
schizophrenia-as-spiritual-emergency. Accessed 3/17/2014.

Huxley, Aldous. (1954). Doors to Perception. U.K.: Chatto-Windus

Idler, Ellen. (2008). The Psychological and Physical Benefits of

Spiritual/Religious Practices. *Spirituality in Higher Education Newsletter.* February, 2008. Volume 4, Issue 2.

James, R.K., and Gilliland, B.E. (1995). *Crisis intervention strategies.* Belmont, CA: Thomson.

James, William (1902). *The varieties of religious experience: A study in human nature.* New York: Longman, Green.

James, William. (1978). Cambridge: Harvard University Press.

James, William. (1988). *Manuscript Lectures.* Cambridge: Harvard University Press.

James, William. "Human immortality: Two supposed objections to the doctrine," in G. Murphy and R.O. Ballou (eds.), *William James on Psychical Research* New York: Viking, 1960, 279-308. Original work delivered as a lecture in 1898.

Jung, C.G. (1958). R.F.C. Hull, translator. *Flying Saucers: A Modern Myth of Things Seen in the Skies.* New York: Harcourt Brace.

Jung, C.G. (1964). Approaching the unconscious. In C.G. Jung (Ed) *Man and his symbols.* London: Aldus Books.

Jung, C.G. in *The Practical Use of Dream Analysis* (1934) quoted in Powell, 25

Jung, C.G. (1970). *Psychology and Religion: West and East. Collected Works of Jung.* Volume 11. Princeton, NJ: Princeton University Press

Jung, C.G. "Commentary on 'The Secret of the Golden Flower,'" Collected Works 13, para. 54, *Alchemical Studies (Collected Works of C.G. Jung, Volume 13)* p. 37. Translated by J.F.C. Hull Bollingen Series xx Princeton University Press, 1983.

Kalweit, H. (1989) When Insanity is a Blessing: The Message of Shamanism. In Grof and Grof (1989) eds. Pp. 77-97

Kane, B. (2005). Spiritual emergency and spiritual emergence: differentiation and interplay. Ann Arbor: MI: Proqust Information and Learning Company.

Kennedy, John F. Quoted at www.goodreads.com/.../1487-the-chinese-use-two-brush-strokes. Accessed 4/28/2014.

Kersting, Karen. (2003, Dec) Religion and Spirituality in the treatment room. American Psychological Association   Monitor. Vol 34, No. 11 http://www.apa.org/monitor/dec03/religion.aspx

Kohr, RL. Near-death experience and its relationship to psi and various altered states. *Theta,* 1982, 10, 50-53.

Kramer, Heinrich and Sprenger, Joseph. *Malleus Maleficarum,* 1487

Kroenke, K. and A.D. Mangelsdorff. (1989). Common Symptoms in

Ambulatory Care: Incidence, Evaluation, Therapy and
Outcome. *American Journal of Medicine* 86: 262-66.

Krupitsky, E., A. Burakov, T. Romanova, I. Dunaevsky, R. Strassman and
A. Grineko (1992) Ketamine Psychotherapy for Heroin
Addiction: Immediate Effects and Two Year Follow-Up.
Journal of Substance Abuse Treatment 23(4): 273-283.

"Kundalini Casualties" *The New Age Journal*, March 1978, p. 47.

Laber-Warren, Emily. (May/June 2013). "The Shroom Shift: Using
psychedelic drugs even once can spark long-lasting changes.
P*sychology Today,* pp. 35-37.

Laing, R.D. (1969) The Divided Self: An Existential Study in Sanity and
Madness. London: Penguin.

Lannert, J. (1991). Resistance and countertransference issues with
spiritual and religious clients. *Journal of Humanistic
Psychology*, 331 (4), 68-76.

Larson, D., Hohmann, A., Kessler, L., Meador, K., Boyd, J., and
McSherry, E. (1988). The couch and the cloth: The
need for linkage. *Hospital and Community Psychiatry,* 39 (10),
1064-1069.

Larson, David (2005). In Jeff Levin and Harold G. Koenig, eds., Faith,
Medicine, and Science: A Festscrift in Honor of Dr. David B.
Larson. New York: Haworth

Leary, Timothy (1969) The Effects of Consciousness-Expanding Drugs
on Prisoner Rehabilitation. *Psychedelic Review* 10:29-45.
http://www.maps.org/psychedelicreview/n10/n10029lea.pdf
Accessed 7/22/2013.

Leary, Timothy. *The Politics of Ecstasy*. Ronin Publishing: Berkeley,
1990

Levin, Jeff and Harold G. Koening, eds., *Faith, Medicine, and Science: A
Festscrift in Honor of Dr. David B. Larson*. New York: Haworth,
2005, p. 19)

Levy, Paul (2009) Possession: ideas inspired by Jung: Beyond Beds:
Alternatives to Psychiatry. http://beyondmeds.com
/com/2009/10/4/possession

Lewis, Sara H. Ayahuasca and Spiritual Crisis: Liminality as Space for
Personal Growth. *Anthropology of Consciousness,* Vol. 19,
Issue 2, pp. 109-133, ISSN 1053-4202, (2008). Pp. 109 – 132.

Lindemann, E. (1944). Symptomatology and management of acute
grief. *American Journal of Psychiatry*, 101, 141-148.

Love, Kristopher. (2014) What a Shaman sees in a mental hospital.
Spirit Science June 16, 2014. http:// the spiritscience.net

/2014/06/16/what-a-shaman-sees-in-a-mental-hospital
Accessed 6/18/2014.

Lucas, M. (2005) On Not Passing the Acid Test: Bad Trips and Initiation. Anthropology of Consciousness 16(1): 25-45.

Ludwig, Arnold (1969). Altered States of Consciousness. In C.T. Tart (ed.) *Altered States of Consciousness.* Pp. 13-19. London: John Wiley & Sons.

Luhrmann, T. (2000) Of Two Minds: The Growing Disorder in American Psychiatry. New York: Alfred A. Knopf

Lukoff, D. (1985). Diagnosis of Mystical Experiences with Psychotic Features. *Journal of Transpersonal Psychology.* 17 (2), 155-8.

Lukoff, D. (March, 1988). The SEN Hotline: Results from a telephone survey. *SEN Newsletter.*

Lukoff, D. (1991) Divine Madness: Shamanistic Initiatory Crisis and Psychosis. Shaman's Drum 22: 24-29.

Lukoff, D. (1998) From Spiritual Emergency to Spiritual Problem: The Transpersonal Roots of the New DSM-IV Category. Journal of Humanistic Psychology 38 (2): 21-50.

Lukoff, D. (2007) Visionary spiritual experience. *Southern Medical Journal* 100 (6), 635-641.

Lukoff, D., Wallace, C.J., Liberman, R.P., & Burke, K. (1986). A holistic program for chronic schizophrenic patients. *Schizophrenia Bulletin,* 12(2), 274-282.

Luna, L.E. and S.F. White (2000) Ayahuasca Reader: Encounters with the Amazon's Sacred Vine. Santa Fe, NM: Synergetic Press.

Mabit, J. (2002) Blending Traditions: Using Indigenous Medicinal Knowledge to Treat Drug Addiction. MAPS   Bulletin 12(2): 25-32.

MacLean, K., J. Johnson, and R. Griffiths. 2011. "Mystical experiences occasioned by the hallucinogen psilocybin lead to increases in the personality domain of openness." *Journal of Psycho-pharmacology.* DOI: 10.1177/0269881111420188.

Marinoff, Lou. (1999). *Plato, not Prozac: Applying eternal wisdom to everyday problems.* HarperCollins, Philadelphia

Marling, Roderick. 2014. The Cannabis Papers: The Sacramental Use of Cannabis Sativa. http://www.Kamakala.com/cannabis.htm.

Martin, Laura. "Eskimo Words for Snow: A Case Study in the Genesis and Decay of an Anthropological Example." *American Anthropologist* vol. 88, No. 2, June 1986.

Maslow, A.H. (1954). *Motivation and personality.* New York: Harper

Maslow, A. (1964). *Religions, Values, and Peak Experiences.* Cleveland,

OH: Ohio State University.

Maslow, A.H. (1970). "Religious Aspects of Peak-Experiences." In
Sadler, W. A. (1970).

Maslow, A. (1971). *The farther reaches of human nature.* New York:
Viking Press.

May, Gerald. *The Dark Night of the Soul: A Psychiatrist Explores the
Connection Between Darkness and Spiritual Growth.*
HarperCollins: NY, 2005

McKenna, Dennis J. Clinical investigations of the therapeutic potential
of ayahuasca: rationale and regulatory challenges.
Pharmacology & Therapeutics 102 (2004) 111-129.
www.sciencedirect.com Accessed 7/23/2014.

McKenna, Terence. (1988). *Food of the Gods.* London: Rider.

McKenna, Terence. (1992). *The Archaic Revival: Speculations on
Psychedelic Mushrooms, the Amazon, Virtual Reality, UFOs,
Evolution, Shamanism, the Rebirth of the Goddess, and the
End of History.* Harper: San Francisco.

Menninger von Leachenthal, Erich (1948). "Death from Psychic Causes.
Bulletin of the Menninger Clinic. 12: 31-36.

Mookerjee, Ajit. (1986). *Kundalini The Arousal of the Inner Energy.*
Destiny Books: Rochester, VT

Murphy, Annie. (Jan/Feb 2011). "Acid Trip: In Search of the Amazon
Magical Mystery Cure". *The Atlantic.* Pp. 23-26.

Narby, J. (1998) The Cosmic Serpent: DNA and the Origins of
Knowledge. New York: Jeremy P. Tarcher/Putnam.
NASW Standards for Cultural Competence in Social Work
Practice. (2001), NASW.

Nelson, J. (1994). *Healing the Spirit.* State University of New York
Press.

Neumann, Erich. (1964) Mystical Man. In Campbell, J. (Ed.) (1969) *The
mystic vision.* Princeton, NJ: Princeton University Press.

Newberg, Andrew; Eugene D'Aquili, and Vince Rause. (2001).
*Why God Won't Go Away: Brain Science and the Biology of
Belief.* New York: Ballantine Books

Osis, K., and Haraldsson, E. *At the Hour of Death.* New York: Avon,
1977.

Otto, Rudolf. *The Idea of the Holy. (Das Heilige.* 1917. English
translation by John W. Harvey, 1924 London: Oxford
University Press

Pahnke, W.N. (1966). Drug and Mysticism. *Internal Journal of
Parapsychology* 8(2): 295-315.

244

Pahnke, W.N. and Richards, W.E. (1966). "Implications of LSD and
Experimental Mysticism." *Journal of Religion and
Health* 5:175.

Parker, Adrian. "We ask, does psi exist? But is this the right question
and do we really want an answer anyway?" in
James E. Alcock, Jean E. Burns, and Anthony Freeman (eds.),
Psi Wars: Getting to Grips with the Paranormal
(Charlottesville, VA: Imprint Academic, 2003, 111-34.

Peck, M. Scott. (1978). *The Road Less Traveled: A New Psychology of
Love, Traditional Values and Spiritual Growth.* New York:
Simon and Schuster.

Phillips, Jonathan Talat. "What Jennifer Aniston May Not Know About
Ayahuasca". *Reality Sandwich http://www.huggingtonpost.
com/jonathan-talat-phillips/jennifer-aniston-and-ayahuasca
-explained_b_1013999.html. Accessed 3/14/2014.*

Pinchbeck, D. (2003). Breaking Open the Head: A Psychedelic Journey
into the Heart of Contemporary Shamanism. New York:
Broadway.

Planck, Max. Wikiquote. en.wikiquote/wiki/Max_Planck. Accessed
6/16/2014.

Plante, T.G. (2009). *Spiritual practices in psychotherapy.* Washington,
D.C..: American Psychological Association.

Pollan, Michael. *The Botany of Desire*. G.K. Hall and Co.: Waterville,
Maine, 2001

Powell, Diane Hennacy. *The ESP Enigma: The Scientific Case for Psychic
Phenomena* Walker & Company: New York

Purdom, C.B. (1964). *The God-man: The Life, Journeys and Work of
Meher Baba.* London: George Allen & Unwin, LTD

Radin, Dean *Entangled Minds: Extrasensory Experiences in a Quantum
Reality* New York: Pocket Books, 2006

Redwood, Daniel. "Interview with Stanislav Grof" Frontiers of the
Mind. www.healthynet/scr/interview.asps?Id= 200. Accessed
3/10/2014

Rees, W.D. "The Hallucinations of Widowhood." *British Medical
Journal* 210:37-41 (1971)

Regehr, C. (2001). Crisis debriefing groups for emergency responders:
reviewing the evidence. *Brief Treatment and Crisis
Intervention*, 1, 87-100.

Rhine, Louisa E. *The Invisible Picture: A Study of Psychic Experiences*
Jefferson, NC: McFarland, 1981

Riba, J., P. Anderer, F. Jane, B. Saletu and M.J. Barbanoj. (2004) Effects of the South American Psychoactive Beverage Ayahuasca on Regional Brain Electrical Activity in Humans: A Functional Neuroimaging Study Using Low-Resolution Electromagnetic Tomography. N europsychobiology 50(1): 89-101.

Ring, K. 1976. *Roots of Renewal in Myth and Madness*. San Francisco, CA: Jossey-Bates Publishers

Ring, K. 1981. Paranormal and other non-ordinary aspects of near-death experiences: Implications for a new paradigm. *Essence,* 5, 33-51.

Ring, K. 1982. Precognitive and prophetic visions in near-death experiences. *Anabiosis,* 2, 47-74.

Ring, K. 1982. *Life at Death: A Scientific Investigation of the Near-Death Experience.* New York: Quill.

Ring, K. 1985. *Heading Toward Omega: In Search of the Meaning of the Near-Death Experience.* New York: Quill

Ring, K. 1998. *Trials of the Visionary Mind: Spiritual Renewal and the Renewal Process.* Albany, NY: State University of New York (SUNY) Press.

Ring, K. and Valerino, E.E. 1998. *Lessons from the Light: What We Can Learn from the Near-Death Experience.* New York: Plenum Press.

Ring, K. and Cooper, S. 1999. *Mindsight: Near-Death and Out-of-Body Experiences in the Blind.* Palo Alto, CA: William James Center for Consciousness Studies.

Roberts, Thomas B. Do entheogen-induced mystical experiences boost the immune system? Psychedelics, peak experiences, and wellness. *Advances in Mind-Body Medicine,* 15 (1999). Reprinted in maps, volume IX, number 3, 1999, pp. 23-25

Rolland, Romain. (1979). *The Life of Ramakrishna*. Vol 1. Calcutta, India: Advaita Ashrama.

Rug, D. Scott. *The Infinite Boundary: A psychic look at Spirit Possession Madness, and Multiple Personality.* Dodd, Mead and Company: New York, 1987

Rush, John A. (Ed.) (2013). *Entheogens and the Development of Culture: The Anthropology and Neurobiology of Ecstatic Experience.* Berkeley, CA: North Atlantic Books.

Ryan, M.B. (2008). The transpersonal William James. *Journal of Transpersonal Psychology,* 40(1), 20-40.

Sabom, M.B. The near-death experience: Myth or reality? A methodological approach. *Anabiosis,* 1981, 1, 44-56.

Sabom, M.B. (1982). *Recollections of Death: A Medical Investigation.*

New York: Harper and Row.

Sadler, W.A. (1970). *Personality and Religion*. New York: Harper & Row.

Sansome, R., Khatain, K., and Rodenhauser, P. (1990). The role of religion in psychiatric education: A national survey. *Academic Psychiatry*, 14, 34-38.

Schwarz, Berthold. *Parent-Child Telepathy* New York: Garrett Publications, 1971

Seligman, M.E.P., & Csikszentmihalyi, M. (2000) Positive Psychology: An introduction. *American Psychologist, 55, 5-14.*SEN@CIIS. Treatment – Types of Spiritual Emergencies http://www. spiritualcompetency.com/se/dxtx/typesose.html Accessed 5/15/2014

Shafranske, E., and Maloney, H. (1990). Clinical psychologists' religious and spiritual orientations and their practice of psycho-therapy. *Psychotherapy*, 27, 72-78.

Shanon, B. (2002) The Antipodes of the Mind: Charting the Phenomenology of the Ayahuasca Experience. New York: Oxford University Press.

Sherwood, J.N., Stolaroff, M.J., and Harman, W.W. (1962). The Psychedelic Experience—A New Concept In Psychotherapy. *J. Neuropsychiat. 4, 69-80*

Shultes, R.E., Hoffmann, A., Ratsch, C. (1992) *Plants of the Gods: Their Sacred, Healing, and Hallucinogenic Powers*. Rochester, VT: Healing Arts Press.

Sidgwick, Henry, et al "Report on the Census of Hallucinations" *Proceedings of the Society for Psychical Research* 6:259-394 (1897)

Siegal, Ronald K. (1980). "Jungle Revelers" *Omni (March 1989)*

Silverman, J. (1967). Shamans and active schizophrenia. American Anthropologist, 69(1), 21-31.

Sinclair, Upton. *Mental Radio* Charlottesville, VA: Hampton Roads Publishing, 2001

"So-called 'Shizophrenia' as Intense Transpersonal or Spiritual Experience: Transformation Process, Spiritual Awakening or 'Spiritual Emergence'. www/jp;ostocedicatpr/com/ spiritualemergence.htm Accessed 8/17/2014.

Sorrell, Stefanie. *Depression As A Spiritual Journey*. John Hunt Publishing: UK, 2009

Sternberg, E.M. *The Balance Within: The Science Connecting Health and Emotions*. New York, NY: W.H. Freeman and Co., 2000

Smith, Daniel B. *Muses, Madmen, and Prophets: Rethinking The History, Science, and Meaning of Auditory Hallucination* The Penguin Press: New York, 2007

Strawbridge, W.J., Cohen, R.D., Shema, S.J. and Kaplan, G.A. (1977). Frequent Attendance at Religious Services and Mortality over 28 Years. *American Journal of Public Health 87: 957-961.*

Szasz, T. (1961) The Myth of Mental Illness: Foundations of a Theory of Personal Conduct. New York: Hoeber-Harper.

Szasz, Thomas. The Myth of Mental Illness Harper Row: New York, 1977

Tartokovsky, M. (2011). 6 Facts About Transpersonal Psychology. *Psych Central* Retrieved March 19, 2014. From http://psychcentral.com/blog/archives/2011/11/03/6-facts-about-transpersonal-psychology/

Tien, A.Y. "Distributions of Hallucinations in the Population." *Social Psychiatry and Psychiatric Epidemiology* 26: 287-92 (1991)

Tarico, Valerie. (2013, March). Religious Trauma Syndrome: How Some Organized Religion Leads to Mental Health Problems. http://awaypoint.wordpress.com/2013/03/26/religious-trauma: syndrome. Accessed7/22/2014.

The Courage to Heal Debunked. N.D.Stopbadtherapy.com/courage/Intro.shtml. Accessed 8/12/2014.

Turner, V. (1967) The Forest of Symbols: Aspects of Ndembu Ritual. Ithaca, NY: Cornell University Press.

Underhill, Evelyn. *Mysticism: A Study in the Nature and Development of Man's Spiritual Consciousness. New York: New American Library, 1974*

Van Lommel, P. "About the Continuity of Our Consciousness." In *Brain Death and Disorders of Consciousness.* Edited by Calixto Machado and D. Alan Shewmon. New York: Kluwer Academic/Plenum, 2004

Victor, Jeffrey S. Moral panics and the social construction of deviant behavior: a theory and application to the case of ritual child abuse. Sociological Perspectives Fall/1998. http://www/love andliberation/info/articlesmoral_panics/htm. Accessed 1/4/2012

Wallace, J.M. and Forman, T. (1998). Religion's role in promoting health and reducing risk among American youth. *Health Education and Behavior* 25: 721-741.

Walsh, R. and Roche, L. (1979) Precipitation of acute psychotic episodes by intensive meditation in individuals with a history of schizophrenia. *American Journal of Psychiatry*, 136, 1085-1086.

Wasson, R. Gordon, Albert Hoffmann, Carl A.P. Ruck. *The Road to Eleusis*. North Atlantic Books

Wasson, R. (2013). Gordon; Khramrisch, Stella; Ott, Jonathan; and Ruck, Carl A.P. (1986). *Persephone's Quest: Entheogens and the Origins of Religion*. Privately Printed.

Watts, Alan. *The Joyous Cosmology: Adventures in the Chemistry of Consciousness*. Novato, CA: New World Library.

Weil, Andrew (1972) *The Natural Mind – A New Way of Looking at Drugs and Higher Consciousness*. Boston: Houghton Mifflin.

Wiger, D.E. and Harowski, K.J. (2003). *Essentials of Crisis Counseling and Intervention*. Hoboken, NJ: John Wiley and Sons.

Wilbert, Johannes. (1987) *Tobacco and Shamanism in South America*. New Haven and London: Yale University Press.

Wilson, W. and Jung, C.G. (1963). Letters. Republished in Grof, S. (Ed.) "Mystical Quest, Attachment, and Addiction. Special Edition of the *Re-Vision Journal* 10 (2): 1987.

Winell, Marlene. (1994) *Leaving the Fold – A Guide for Former Fundamentalists and Others Leaving Their Religion*. New Harbinger Publishers: Oakland, CA, 1994.

Winkelman, Michael. *Psychointegration: The Physiological Effects of Entheogens*. Site Street. Spring 2003. http://www/maps.org /media/windelman-spring03/html. Accessed 7/22/2013.

Winkelman, M. (2001) Alternative and Traditional Medicine Approaches for Substance Abuse Programs: A Shamanic Perspective. International Journal of Drug Policy 12 (4): 337-351.

CPSIA information can be obtained at www.ICGtesting.com
Printed in the USA
BVOW04s1941050515

399088BV00016B/309/P